Journaling WITH The LORD

CYNTHIA LOCKE-HENDERSON

JayMedia
Publishing

ISBN: 978-1-95744305-8

First printing, 2022.

JayMedia Publishing
Laurel, MD 20708

www.publishing.jaymediagroup.net

Forward

Dr. Cynthia L. Henderson is a phenomenal woman, mother, writer, and poet who have written from her personal experiences and through the inspiration of God. She has been chosen to live through her experiences by God so that her legacy will encourage and strengthen others. It was no mistake that she endured the challenges in her life. God designed her life as if it was a Picasso painting that hangs in the museum of life so that others may be blessed over a life time and see that there is hope in the outcome of any situation. Her accomplishments have been noted through the lives of her children, family, and friends. Through her journey, God has made it known through her daily devotions that are inspired by Him through her that it's not over and that it has just begun. How do I know? I'm her sister and she inspires me daily with a word from our heavenly father. I love you my beautiful sister!

"Trisha"
Patricia V. Wilson

Preface

My morning time with the Lord has become a relationship building time between the two of us. I write to Him and He answers back. I pray for personal healing and the healing of others. God gives me situations that need my attention. It comes out in the writing and in the scriptures that He gives to support what I have written.

This continues to be a powerful time. I am fully aware that my gift is not for me alone. That is why I delight in writing for God. Sometimes the messages are so strong that I weep with a surrendering spirit. I weep when I am compelled to dig deep within myself to release the scars from my past. I weep for the challenges of others. I weep out of reverence for my almighty, compassionate, deliberate, excellent, compelling, faithful and forgiving God.

I have been without a lot of things in life; however, I have NEVER been without God. **This gift of writing has been with me from my childhood to this present day. Despite all that I have been through, God has never taken this gift away from me.**

All scripture references are New International Version (NIV), unless otherwise noted

There is always hope when
everything around you is dying.

As we began increasing the time talking to God, lets first detox or empty out:

Every doubt
Every sinful thought
Every useless thought
Every painful thought
Every power draining thought
Every progress stopping thought
Every "I can't do this" thought

This is needed as we make room for the courage that the Lord is going to give us as we really talk to Him. Let's make room for the Lord to give us His plans and directions for moving FORWARD.

<u>Empty Out:</u>

- Worrying about my children (grandchildren) issues. (You've got them Lord; I need to get out of the way).

- Trying to figure out my future when I haven't finished with the present. My presents (gifts) include: Every day you allow me to wake and participate in my day. I have 4 wonderful children and 6 grands. You have allowed me to retire with sustainable provisions and you used one of those wonderful children to help me. You anoint my printed thoughts. Lord, thank you for all that you give.

- Fear. You place MANY projects in my mind and heart to help others and to show your glory. I need you to give me courage to walk into my present season.

- Fear of being accepted by others. You have given me acceptance where I need it and with whom I need it. I want to shift my focus to worshiping you when I feel unaccepted.

- Fear and lack of boldness when I need to stand up.

- Irrelevant histories that often torment my thoughts.

Contents

Forward   iii

Preface   v

The Battle Of Peace And Worry   1

You Are Artistic Lord   3

Water Is Essential For Life   5

Paths   7

Less I Forget Calvary   9

Your Majesty   11

Thank You For My Girl   13

Just Try Him   15

Wait   17

Be Still   19

The Power In Waiting   21

Great Is Your Faithfulness   23

I Can't Imagine   25

The Lord Is My Shepherd   27

Just Pray   29

The Chastisement Of Our Peace Was Upon Him   32

Give Me You Lord   35

Heart To Heart, Word To Word, Pen To Paper   37

Lord, You Are Just One Scripture Away   39

Lord, You Have Done It Just For Me   41

Lord Forgive   44

Lord You Repaired My Broken Road   46

You Give Strength Every Cycle   49

Lord I Thank You   51

Oh, For Your Grace   53

I Am Entering Your Gates Lord   55

Appreciativeness   57

Lord, I Can't Identify This Emptiness – Help!   59

What Is Time That Thou Art Mindful Of   61

Secret Place   63

Forgiveness (My Rainbow Promise)   65

Why Did It Take So Long? 68

I Skipped My Time With You 71

My Timing Is Not Your Timing 73

Lord My Hands Write What My Heart Speaks 75

What Is Blocking The Door? 77

Take A Bird's Point Of View 80

Focus 82

Healing Is Needed 84

Danger All Around 86

On My Way To Here 89

God Has Your Answers, Listen As His Words Speak 91

You Blessed My Seeds 94

Thank You For An Upgrade 97

It Is Another Day, And The Lord Has Kept Me 99

I Have Purpose 102

Modify And Move Forward 105

The Answer 108

You Had To Do It And I Am Glad 110

Victory When Unfairness Isn't Fair 113

Lord, Thank You For Remembering The Good 115

Light My Way, You See What I Can't See 119

Broken To Be Made Whole 122

Many Things Die Lord, But You Refused To Die Permanently 125

I Am There In So Many Ways 128

Above All I Have, I See You, Lord 130

My Anticipation Is YOU 133

There Is Nothing To Be Said Except Thank You 136

You Raised Me Up Beyond Mountains 138

My Help Comes From You Lord 141

I Am Enough 144

Where Would I Be If It Were Not For You Lord 146

The Lord Is My Conductor 149

You Are There Every Time 152

Lord, You Opened Doors, Help Me Accomplish Your Will 154

Lord, I Belong To You 157

Wonderful Things Happen When You "Be Still" 160

Complexity Fight With Praise 163

Lord I Believe 166

Today Is A New Day 169

Pray 171

You Are Immeasurable 173

I Could Not Make It Without You 176

Miracles Happen Non-Stop   178

Nothing Can Keep My God Away from Me   181

Have I Told You Lately, How Much I Love You   184

You Are My Source   187

Why Should I Feel Discouraged?   189

Life is Like A Spiral   192

You Are God Alone And There is None Comparable   195

Thanks Giving   198

I Can't Fill The Gaps In Life   201

Have I Ignored The Examples Of Baby Jesus?   204

Your Life Was Given Without A Price Tag, So Are Your Blessings   207

Jesus An Unimaginable Wonder   210

The Gift That Keeps Giving   213

Be It Unto Me   216

The Gift We Really Need Is Not Under The Tree   219

Transitioned For Us   222

How Excellent Is Your Name In All The Earth   225

Thanks For Making Me, Me   228

I Saw You, When You Did Not See Me   231

Unforgiveness Attempted To Stop Baby Jesus' Birth Plans   234

Jesus' Birth Demonstrated Lessons In Obedience   237

Unto Us A Son Is Given   240

Born To Know Us Inside And Out   243

Don't Leave Your Gift Under The Tree   246

He Came Because Of Love   249

From Human To Divine   252

The Party Is Over And You Are Still Giving   255

Lord You Are Consistent   258

"Keep Me Looking Up And Moving Forward!"   261

I Am Nothing Without You   264

New Year, New Chance To Make Different Decisions   267

Options   270

One Ounce Of Faith Is What Fuels My Hope In Christ   273

Lord Can I Be "STRAIGHTFORWARD" With You   276

Change Your Language   279

Abide   282

In Between Time   285

Invisible Blessings   288

Lord You Can Read Me Inside And Out   290

My Heart Needs Intervention From You   293

You Chose Me   295

Reveal Me To Me   297

Lord I Need "Leveling Out"   300

Lord I Am Sorry For Ignoring Your Presence   303

The Plot   306

Lord I Need An Answer   309

There Was A Second Set Of Footprints Next To Mine In The Footprints Of Time   312

Thanks For Bringing Light To My Dark Places   315

Time Does Not Belong To Me   318

I Need Heart Surgery   320

I Am Living Because Of Mercy   322

I Am Confident That You Are Molding Me   325

Wait On The Lord   328

A Bag Of Wants Can Cause Devastation   331

You Waited   334

My Level Of Trust Is Equal To My Response To God   336

PUSH   339

Lord, Search My Heart And Thoughts   342

Lord Teach Me Your Way   344

Cry Out To God For Purpose   346

PTT Me (Prove, Try, Test)   348

Daddy The Road Has So Many Turns, Crack, And Holes   350

Lord, I Find Myself "Here". Help!   352

Here I Am   355

Interruptions   357

See Me, Show Me, Help Me   359

Whining Does Not Help   361

Legacy   363

Light   365

The Value Of My Days   367

God, Send Me   369

God You Never Stopped Loving Me   371

You Love Me Enough To Die For Me   373

Lump Of Clay   375

I Am Getting Old, But I Still Have Some Strength Left   377

Choosing God's Path   379

Contentment With God   381

Lord, I Hear You   384

Lord My Faith Without You Won't Work   386

Afterword   388

Scripture Reference Versions   389

The Battle Of Peace And Worry

(ISAIAH 26:3)

It is all in your mind this battle of peace and worry.
You try within yourself because you want it to go in a hurry.
My efforts bring only things that seek to destroy this temple that God
has created.
My efforts only add to what exist and makes me more weighted.

Oh Lord it seems so difficult to let this basket of worry go and not return.
Oh Lord please help me to see that yielding to worry takes away all that
I learn.
When I don't trust in you, I throw away the peace you have given me.
Lord let me see that worrying puts a gap in the relationship between me
and thee.

I need to hold on to your promise that the world does not understand
and cannot give.
You invite me to trust you and not allow my heart to be troubled, you
invite me to live.
Lord help me regulate the thoughts in my mind and heart, because I am
as my heart reasons.
Your peace has recused repeatedly, so dominate me with your peace for
this present season.

Written during my time with God reflecting on his skillful management of worry.
Dr. Cynthia Locke Henderson3/31/19©

God's word is powerful. What does this scripture say to you?

_____

_____

_____

_____

_____

What have you learned during this time with Lord?

_____

_____

_____

_____

_____

Are there things you need to do differently?

_____

_____

_____

_____

_____

Before you leave this moment, write down God's directions to you.

_____

_____

_____

_____

_____

Close this journaling moment with a prayer.

_____

_____

_____

_____

_____

You Are Artistic Lord

(PSALM 139:14)

Lord you are quiet the artist of all things beautiful and
limitless shades of color in the world around us
The sparrow does not complain about its size compared to other birds
and accepts diversity in color with a fuss
Lord why does man use his color diversity to contemplate ways to be
greater than the others
It is almost like the separation at the tower of Babel, where similarities
separated likeness of sisters and brothers

I look at the diversity and plight of a tree and its ability to stand whether
tall, short, bruised, broken, bent
Then Lord, I look at man and consider how life has given joy for some
and destruction for others ill intent
Similar to the tree, Lord you help us weather storms, bend but not break,
lose leaves, that return in the spring
Lord you give abundantly to those called your heirs, like ponds that flow
into rivers and become bigger things

Only you God could design so much with the color yellow, hang the sun,
spread the pedals of the sunflower
Only you God could create a yellow butterfly that emerges from an
unsightly cocoon at just the right hour
You created man with diversity in color, size, wisdom, talents, cultures,
yet with so many possibilities
Lord help me, help us to appreciate your beauty and fulfill your plans for
us and know our responsibilities

Written during my time with God reflecting on his artistry and design of this world.
Dr. Cynthia Locke Henderson3/31/19©

3

✏ God's word is powerful. What does this scripture say to you?

_____

_____

_____

_____

_____

✏ What have you learned during this time with Lord?

_____

_____

_____

_____

_____

✏ Are there things you need to do differently?

_____

_____

_____

_____

_____

✏ Before you leave this moment, write down God's directions to you.

_____

_____

_____

_____

_____

✏ Close this journaling moment with a prayer.

_____

_____

_____

_____

_____

Water Is Essential For Life

(ISAIAH 41:18)

Lord there have been times in my life when all around me seems dry.
There is nothing to give me an explanation for this dryness or a reason why.
During this drought friends and resources seem limited and sometimes non-existing.
Aloneness takes over and thinking that I matter to no one is a feeling that's persisting.

You blessed me with family and I thank you for each one of them.
Lord in this dry season, they are not there, they are stored away like a treasured gem.
I thirst for your water that washes away the cracks and brokenness in me before too long.
Lord this I know is the test that helps me know that when I am weak, then I am strong.

Lord I come to you because you can fill the cracks and mend my broken place.
Lord bring restoration, inspire my soul, and influence my thoughts with your divine grace.
Where your spirit is, there is liberty like a river of life flowing through my hurt.
You Lord send rivers in bare places, springs in the midst of valleys, pools in my desert

Written during my time with the Lord on 4/1/2019 praying for me and another.
Dr. Cynthia Locke Henderson©

God's word is powerful. What does this scripture say to you?

_____

_____

_____

_____

What have you learned during this time with Lord?

_____

_____

_____

_____

Are there things you need to do differently?

_____

_____

_____

_____

Before you leave this moment, write down God's directions to you.

_____

_____

_____

_____

Close this journaling moment with a prayer.

_____

_____

_____

_____

_____

Paths

(PROVERB 3:5,6)

Paths in our lives lead us to many directions
Often the paths are sought because we want certain connections
The paths that we choose thinking it's best for us, we really believe that
with all our might
However, the consequences of that path cause us to manipulate trying to
make it right

Paths we travel take us into situations that cause regrets, bitterness, and
fear
Despite our selections, you my God are always watching and waiting and
you stand near
Our determination eliminates keeping God in the process and takes to
disappointments
We find ourselves way behind where we were meant to be - missing
God's appointments

Lord, I commit to the paths you have laid out to for me, so that I author
good stories
Paths that lead me to your purpose to bless me and expand my
territories
Lord, I now see that you want a relationship that allows me to be who
you want me to be
Lord, I am not perfect, but every day I will take the time to worship and
praise thee

Written as I made time for God who always has time for me.
Dr. Cynthia Locke Henderson ©4/3/2019

God's word is powerful. What does this scripture say to you?

_____

_____

_____

_____

_____

What have you learned during this time with Lord?

_____

_____

_____

_____

_____

Are there things you need to do differently?

_____

_____

_____

_____

_____

Before you leave this moment, write down God's directions to you.

_____

_____

_____

_____

_____

Close this journaling moment with a prayer.

_____

_____

_____

_____

_____

Less I Forget Calvary

(ROMANS 5:8, 6:10)

Most of my life, I am told of the story of the crucifixion and your death
I am reminded how others cheered for your death laced with intense
hatred wealth
I am reminded of the struggle you had carrying your own cross
Some cried, but there were those that hated so much that anything they
would toss

Lord today, so many years after such a great sacrifice some actions say
crucify him
Our life of sin is like swinging the whip that beat his body limb by limb
You could have, but you did not get off the cross to free yourself, that
was not the plan
Today the story is told in plays, movies and sermons, yet our sins, kill
the man

How much more does it take for us to realize the sacrifice and the beginning of grace
I can only imagine the sadness he feels when we refuse redemption and
sin we embrace
I am in awe of the beatings you took for me to be free, redeemed, and
made your heir
After all that man did to you, you still loved us, no matter you continue
showing you care

Written during my time before my Majestic and all-Powerful God,
Dr. Cynthia Locke Henderson ©3/7/2019

God's word is powerful. What does this scripture say to you?

_____

_____

_____

_____

_____

What have you learned during this time with Lord?

_____

_____

_____

_____

_____

Are there things you need to do differently?

_____

_____

_____

_____

_____

Before you leave this moment, write down God's directions to you.

_____

_____

_____

_____

_____

Close this journaling moment with a prayer.

_____

_____

_____

_____

_____

_____

Your Majesty

(REVELATIONS 4:11)

Lord this day I take time to worship you because you are worthy to receive, glory, honor and power
Lord I bring so many of my cares to you loading you with my concerns, but this is your hour
You know what goes on with me, what causes me difficulty and you fix each one of my complaints
You listen to everyone that comes to you and continue to teach all of your saints how to use restraints

I know you like hearing from us and having conversation with us. You love to hear our calls
Yet I know that you like to hear our thoughts and prayers, pick us up when we have falls
This moment, I leave my thoughts behind and worship you because you, oh Lord, are worthy of praise
You deserve our presentations as living sacrifices; you deserve acknowledgement from us all days

You are our rescuer when we are in our many valley experiences and can't see a way out
You are honored when you respond to our silent tears that no one else can see and when we shout
We look back and are in awe of the distance that you have bought us from and where we now stand
There is none like you, none that takes the time you do to simply hold us in the protection of your hand

My God how majestic, how miraculous, how wonderful,
how unfailing you are, you are always there!

God's word is powerful. What does this scripture say to you?

_____
_____
_____
_____
_____

What have you learned during this time with Lord?

_____
_____
_____
_____
_____

Are there things you need to do differently?

_____
_____
_____
_____
_____

Before you leave this moment, write down God's directions to you.

_____
_____
_____
_____
_____

Close this journaling moment with a prayer.

_____
_____
_____
_____
_____

Thank You For My Girl

—————— ❦ ——————

Today I celebrate a wish I made several years ago. I prayed for a girl
I wanted one that was made just for me and unlike any other one in the
world
I had certain specifications and expectations; you honored every one
I asked for her beauty, smartness and hair on her head, you did it when
all was done

You took her through many roles and life events to make her strong
She learned from everything life threw her way because you watched her
from your throne
She was like my living doll, that I enjoyed making her shine, caring for
her and holding her in my arms
She was silent the day she was born, causing me to wonder if her life was
on a path of harm

They took her away from me to another place for care, those were
moments that hurt even now
Would she be ok, would they know what to do, would her silence go
away, I could not imagine how?
You let her wake up, we never found out why she was silent but it went
away because of your grace.
Now when I look at my family tree, there she is with my first grands in
her own special place

Thank you, Lord, for my little girl who grew up to be a wonderful mom.

Written on the day that I celebrate and thank God for my little girl who is now a lady;
Schnearia by mom Dr. Cynthia Locke Henderson Written ©4/8/2019

✎ God's word is powerful. What does this scripture say to you?

_____

_____

_____

_____

_____

✎ What have you learned during this time with Lord?

_____

_____

_____

_____

_____

✎ Are there things you need to do differently?

_____

_____

_____

_____

_____

✎ Before you leave this moment, write down God's directions to you.

_____

_____

_____

_____

_____

✎ Close this journaling moment with a prayer.

_____

_____

_____

_____

_____

Just Try Him

Trust in the LORD with all thine heart;
and lean not unto thine own understanding.

In all thy ways acknowledge him, and he shall direct thy paths.

(PROV. 3:5-6 KJV)

God sees our thoughts, our heart and everything that we do right or wrong
He sees us when we think we are at our peak in life and feeling strong
Our altitude implies that we reached milestones in our own might and strength
We build our own idols, placing ourselves at the top at any length

Oh, how lost we feel when our "London Bridge" comes falling down
Oh, how lost we feel when self-praise is gone, others don't praise, there is not a sound
Our abilities were given by God, how dare we take recognition and authorship
What are we, who are we, where are we when the cards are flipped?

God writes our stories, he knows the beginning, what happens in the middle and the end
He does not turn against us when we drown in our self-absorbed state of mind
He loves us, forgives us, receives us, shepherds us, teaches us, creates us and elevates us
All he asks of us is, to worship him for his awesomeness and lose ourselves in his trust

*God's love rebuilds us again and again, he loves us,
we must love him back.*

✏ God's word is powerful. What does this scripture say to you?

_____
_____
_____
_____
_____

✏ What have you learned during this time with Lord?

_____
_____
_____
_____
_____

✏ Are there things you need to do differently?

_____
_____
_____
_____
_____

✏ Before you leave this moment, write down God's directions to you.

_____
_____
_____
_____
_____

✏ Close this journaling moment with a prayer.

_____
_____
_____
_____
_____

Wait

But they that wait upon the LORD shall renew their strength; they shall mount up with wings as eagles; they shall run, and not be weary; and they shall walk, and not faint.

(ISAIAH 40:31)

Waiting seems like a hard game to play when we want change to come now
We want what we want, but it seems that God is not responding and will not allow
Life to move in the direction that we want him to move with speed
Wait on the Lord we have heard over and over and have tried to take heed

We cry for the Lord in the middle of a very bad storm, or a hurricane of life event
The sun does come out brighter than ever, shining its light and causing us to repent
Repent for rushing God and realizing that our life could have taking a different direction
Pain and sin could have attacked, our way would have guided us wrong without protection

The Lord saw the person waiting to rip our purposes and possibilities away causing a delay
Lord you have been merciful forgiving our impatience, bringing peace as you mold us your way
Lord there have been times that we should have, we could have lost and everything gone
Lord you allowed us to fall, but taught us to rise above it all and never stopped calling us your own

Written during my time with the Lord, listening to him teach me to WAIT
by Dr. Cynthia Locke Henderson @4/11/2019

God's word is powerful. What does this scripture say to you?

_____

_____

_____

_____

_____

What have you learned during this time with Lord?

_____

_____

_____

_____

_____

Are there things you need to do differently?

_____

_____

_____

_____

_____

Before you leave this moment, write down God's directions to you.

_____

_____

_____

_____

_____

Close this journaling moment with a prayer.

_____

_____

_____

_____

_____

Be Still

Wait for the LORD; be strong and take heart and wait for the LORD.

(PSALM 27:14)

Things happen all around us, there is nothing that we can do, there is
just stillness
There is the absence of feeling that God is not speaking, we feel we have
no access
I stand in the midst of things happening all around me but don't know
what is needed from me
I know you are there; I see things and think that I have to do something
or just let it be

I have learned to stop the worrying because it does not solve anything
It does not make things better, instead it rips away at my peace and
change the song I sing
You have built a fortress around me, but still I see and think about the
unrest outside the wall
Lord, what do I do with this moment of stillness when I feel like duty
has made a call?

Lord, I am reminded that you will remove my weariness, allow me to
walk and not be weak
Lord you and you can restore my strength at a time like this when the
outcomes seem bleak
Lord I am reminded that you promised to meet me where I stand if I
just keep still
For there are times when I must do NOTHING and release myself to
simply follow your will

Peace Be Still

✏ God's word is powerful. What does this scripture say to you?

_____

_____

_____

_____

_____

✏ What have you learned during this time with Lord?

_____

_____

_____

_____

_____

✏ Are there things you need to do differently?

_____

_____

_____

_____

_____

✏ Before you leave this moment, write down God's directions to you.

_____

_____

_____

_____

_____

✏ Close this journaling moment with a prayer.

_____

_____

_____

_____

_____

The Power In Waiting

Yet the Lord longs to be gracious to you;
 therefore, he will rise up to show you compassion.
For the Lord is a God of justice.
 Blessed are all who wait for him! Isaiah 30:18 NIV

We wait in hope for the LORD;
he is our help and our shield. Psalm 33:20

Lamentations 3: 24,25
I say to myself, "The LORD is my portion;
 therefore I will wait for him."
The LORD is good to those whose hope is in him,
 to the one who seeks him;

God's word is powerful. What does this scripture say to you?

_____

_____

_____

_____

_____

What have you learned during this time with Lord?

_____

_____

_____

_____

_____

Are there things you need to do differently?

_____

_____

_____

_____

_____

Before you leave this moment, write down God's directions to you.

_____

_____

_____

_____

_____

Close this journaling moment with a prayer.

_____

_____

_____

_____

_____

Great Is Your Faithfulness

Because of the LORD's great love we are not consumed, for his compassions never fail. They are new every morning; great is your faithfulness.

(LAMENTATIONS 3:22-23)

It free to us when we have done things our way, your mercy is free and not saleable

Lord, I repent this moment for taken your mercy so selfishly and without gratitude for it

Lord, please help me be the person you have called me to be and disobedience I want to quit

Without fail you are there when I speak in anger or fail to give the unconditional love you give me

Lord, help me focus on seeing the wrong in me and not focusing on the wrong in others that I see

It feels so great when you forgive me, I image how great you feel when I can forgive another

We are heirs to you and part of the family, the ones that I do not forgive are my sister or brother

Lord, help not waste any more time on being unforgiving, holding on to the past, and not caring

You rescue us from ourselves not just to do nothing. Make us be available to be loving and sharing

Our anger blocks our thought of the endless mercy you give to use without a monetary price

Lord you are amazing, brilliant, deliberate with your love, infallible, legitimate, God you are nice

Lord help me be some of the things you are to others,
you are my teacher and example!

God's word is powerful. What does this scripture say to you?

_____

_____

_____

_____

_____

What have you learned during this time with Lord?

_____

_____

_____

_____

_____

Are there things you need to do differently?

_____

_____

_____

_____

_____

Before you leave this moment, write down God's directions to you.

_____

_____

_____

_____

_____

Close this journaling moment with a prayer.

_____

_____

_____

_____

_____

I Can't Imagine

No temptation has overtaken you except what is common to mankind.
And God is faithful; he will not let you be tempted beyond what you
can bear. But when you are tempted, he will also provide
a way out so that you can endure it.

(I CORINTHIANS 10:13)

Lord, I can't imagine my life without you, without your love, without
protection
There were times when Satan would attempt to make me feel that in my
life was no affection
There were times when dark clouds seemed to cloud my day and outlook
There were days that I seemed to lose everything, I had stories that could
feel a book

In the midst of my trying circumstances, you gave me hope and strength
through your words
Lost in my learning, you taught me so much that others called me names
associated with nerds
No matter what the plight was, there seemed to be a string that kept me
connected to you
I simply can't imagine my life without ordering my steps in everything
you charged me to do

I'm so glad you saved me for such a day as this day because you had more
You went to every closed door for me and opened door after door, yes
door after door
With every hard thing in my life, you drew me closer to you, you
sustained me
With a bond that no one could break, a relationship just between the
two of us, me and thee

I could not imagine a temptation or test to take me away from you.

God's word is powerful. What does this scripture say to you?

_____

_____

_____

_____

_____

What have you learned during this time with Lord?

_____

_____

_____

_____

_____

Are there things you need to do differently?

_____

_____

_____

_____

_____

Before you leave this moment, write down God's directions to you.

_____

_____

_____

_____

_____

Close this journaling moment with a prayer.

_____

_____

_____

_____

_____

The Lord Is My Shepherd

(PSALM 23)

The 23rd Psalm was taught when were kids. It was a Bible passage we had to learn
We never questioned why we had to learn it, we just prepared to recite it when it was our turn
We played in our neighborhoods with no fear of anything happening to us
Because while we learned the Psalm, we were also taught to believe God's word and in him trust

Today, Lord things have changed for children, their safety is often a common prayer request
They go to school seeking to learn all that they can and bring report cards showing their best
Yet, our children are getting shot to death on their playground, in their homes, in their schools
Drug use and sell cause us to find the older ones, dead lying abandon in their own blood pools

Despite what is happening, I still trust that you are my shepherd who has never left his post
There are births of children, just as there are deaths of children, I don't know which are the most
We have been warned of imminent destruction of life and that these acts are part of the last days
Not reject you shepherding some remain under your protection or leave to be with you always

Lord my ways are not your ways, neither are my thoughts your thoughts, I trust you my Shepherd

Written during my time with the Lord and talking to him about our children
by Dr. Cynthia Locke Henderson @ 4/17/2019

✏ God's word is powerful. What does this scripture say to you?

_____
_____
_____
_____
_____

✏ What have you learned during this time with Lord?

_____
_____
_____
_____
_____

✏ Are there things you need to do differently?

_____
_____
_____
_____
_____

✏ Before you leave this moment, write down God's directions to you.

_____
_____
_____
_____
_____

✏ Close this journaling moment with a prayer.

_____
_____
_____
_____
_____
_____

Just Pray

Ask and it will be given to you; seek and you will find; knock
and the door will be opened to you.

(MATTHEW 7:7)

Call to me and I will answer you and tell you great
and unsearchable things you do not know.

(JEREMIAH 33:3)

There are so many happenings in life that you become overwhelmed
with fear
You wonder if you are worthy to make a request to the Lord – does he
want to hear
You convict yourself and feel God does not do anything for a person like
you
You feel there is too much sin in your life for Him to pay attention to
anything you do

The enemy would have you believe that your past is unforgiveable, you
got a nerve
You believe that the pain you caused to others and now the only thing
you deserve
You make so many excuses instead of presenting your case to the God
for intervention
Your view of your life is too complexed, too crowded with things that
you can't mention

God already knows your secrets; good and bad, everything that you have
ever done
He knows your every thought and action, that is why He gave his one
and only son

God simply wants to hear from you, he delights in caring for you, stop judging yourself

God hears your every word, he knows your need, talk to Him, He is waiting, He is not deaf

Form simple to complex, God does and wants to hear from you.

Written during my time in prayer with the Lord. He answered me before I finished.
Dr. Cynthia Locke Henderson @ 4/18/2019

God's word is powerful. What does this scripture say to you?

_____

_____

_____

_____

_____

What have you learned during this time with Lord?

_____

_____

_____

_____

_____

Are there things you need to do differently?

_____

_____

_____

_____

_____

Before you leave this moment, write down God's directions to you.

_____

_____

_____

_____

_____

Close this journaling moment with a prayer.

_____

_____

_____

_____

_____

The Chastisement Of Our Peace Was Upon Him

But he was pierced for our transgressions, he was crushed for our
iniquities; the punishment that brought us peace was on him,
and by his wounds we are healed.

(ISAIAH 53:5)

Peace is given to us for a price that we could not pay, no substitution
for what was given
After Calvary nothing could we give because death came after the nail
was driven
Blood flowed from Christ to cause healing in our souls and no
retribution for our sin
He gave it up to us to receive his gift of cleansing us from without and
within

We suffer instead of accepting the price, he paid for all that we did to
break ties with the Master
There was no remedy for our suffering, no remedy because our life was
heading for a disaster
The sacrifice of blood that flowed from the thorns, the nails in his hand
and the spear in his side
The pain He felt from stripes, He choose to feel pain as a man before he
gave up life and died

The sacrifice he made give strength when we think we can't make it,
when we can't trust Him
The pain we suffer from sin, the turmoil we endure, we give it all to Him
when all seems so dim

The chastisement of our peace was upon Him as he gave His life on the tree and paid our debts
All afflictions he delivers, all our unrest, all our pain he heals, trust that he removes all threats

God is our strength and portion forever, accept it "freely"

/ God's word is powerful. What does this scripture say to you?

_____

_____

_____

_____

_____

/ What have you learned during this time with Lord?

_____

_____

_____

_____

_____

/ Are there things you need to do differently?

_____

_____

_____

_____

_____

/ Before you leave this moment, write down God's directions to you.

_____

_____

_____

_____

_____

/ Close this journaling moment with a prayer.

_____

_____

_____

_____

_____

Give Me You Lord

Call to me and I will answer you and tell you great
and unsearchable things you do not know.

(JEREMIAH 33:3)

Lord, our "want" list is full of things that don't last
So full of things that are part of our past
We negotiate for more than you have already given to please our desire
We want to do so many things and moving up is what we inspire

Lord, so much of our time is lost not knowing what we should ask
Deep within us is discontentment, longing for temporary things while
hiding behind a mask
Somewhere in the mist of our unrest we realized that we want and need
YOU
Lord, we get tired of others' empty promises, lies that never represent
what is true

Lord, please forgive us for sharing our heart with distractions that so
easily weigh us down
Still you honor your promise of life everlasting with you and someday to
wear your crown
Give more of you to lighten my dark days, to lift me out of deep valleys
and clear my vision
Give more of you in my thoughts, in my daily walk, and in every big or
small chance for decision

Lord, you are truly all I need!

*Written during a refreshing moment with the Lord who is always near to hear me by Dr.
Cynthia Locke Henderson @ 4/24/2019*

God's word is powerful. What does this scripture say to you?

_____

_____

_____

_____

_____

What have you learned during this time with Lord?

_____

_____

_____

_____

_____

Are there things you need to do differently?

_____

_____

_____

_____

_____

Before you leave this moment, write down God's directions to you.

_____

_____

_____

_____

_____

Close this journaling moment with a prayer.

_____

_____

_____

_____

_____

Heart To Heart,
Word To Word, Pen To Paper

———— ❦ ————

Blessed are those who hunger and thirst for righteousness,
for they will be filled.

(MATTHEW 5:6)

Lord, it is not in the loudness of prayer words spoken for others to
hear my heart
Lord, neither is it in how grandiose the words I use to imply that I am smart
It is in the unspoken words and how we exchange thoughts
It is in the things you speak directly to me, Lord they fill my heart's
many empty spots

When I speak to you heart to heart you understand what I want to say
Lord, you take my confusion, my inquiry, my tangled thoughts and
organize them your way
Lord, you make sense of broken places, desolate places, quiet storms
inside of me
I can only mourn not knowing exactly what I want, or where I want to be

Ultimately Lord, the one thing that I know is that I need you more and
more
Despite how good things are, I know you have something I need that is
yearning at my core
You are a God of Justice; you know how to deliberate my decisions in a
way that please you
Lord, you speak oh so silently, yet so powerfully you fill my empty places
with a spiritual glue

Oh, how I love you

*Written during my time with the Lord and not a word spoken, I listened with y heart as he
inspired me. Dr. Cynthia Locke Henderson @4/30/2019*

God's word is powerful. What does this scripture say to you?

_____

_____

_____

_____

_____

What have you learned during this time with Lord?

_____

_____

_____

_____

_____

Are there things you need to do differently?

_____

_____

_____

_____

_____

Before you leave this moment, write down God's directions to you.

_____

_____

_____

_____

_____

Close this journaling moment with a prayer.

_____

_____

_____

_____

_____

Lord, You Are Just One Scripture Away

—————— ❧ ——————

In the silence of the morning and the hush of all vocal distractions you are here
As I wait in anticipation to hear what you have to say for today, I can feel you are near
Jeremiah 33:3 invites me to call because you have great and unsearchable things to share
I feel a void and don't know what to say, but I feel a deeper call saying that you care

Matthews 6:10 admonishes me to repent daily for any thoughts known and unknown
So that I can present myself holy and acceptable as I access your throne
Lord you see me inside and out, you see my blemishes, my unhealed hurts and hear my plea
Lord I trust your word in Deuteronomy 30:3 that says you will restore all taken away from me

James 5:16 tells me the prayer of a righteous person is powerful and effective
When we pray you help us see through your eyes and give us a different perspective
Matthews 19:26 reminds me that some things are impossible for man, yet all things are possible with God
There is power in your word.
Hebrews 4:12 tells us the word of God is alive and active, there is no fraud

Lord you and your word are the real powerful thing

Written as God brought the necessary scripture to my mind. How awesome!
Dr. Cynthia Locke Henderson on @ 5/1/2019

🖊 God's word is powerful. What does this scripture say to you?

_____

_____

_____

_____

🖊 What have you learned during this time with Lord?

_____

_____

_____

_____

🖊 Are there things you need to do differently?

_____

_____

_____

_____

🖊 Before you leave this moment, write down God's directions to you.

_____

_____

_____

_____

🖊 Close this journaling moment with a prayer.

_____

_____

_____

_____

_____

Lord, You Have Done It Just For Me

We wait in hope for the LORD; he is our help and our shield.

(PSALM 33:20)

Lord, I look at where I am today and where I was yester years your direction is evident
I see your hand of love in everything that happened to me, nothing was irrelevant
Each downfall makes me appreciate the rise to your will in my writing, your will in caring
I saw you help my mom multiply little into much and enough for giving to others and sharing

Lord, I witnessed your healing hands as you gave her air when her breathing was compromised
Then you did the same for me as I suffered with asthma, one touch and prayer, healing was authorized
In poverty you exposed me to love, yes endless love, so much of it that at the time I did not realize poverty
Daily opportunity to witness my mom's prayers come true, she showed me the benefits of generosity

Every now and then I miss her but understand she was here long enough to teach me your ways
You knew the road ahead would have challenges, so she taught me to give praise no matter the days
To understand that you had purpose in everything in my life, I now know that you loved me into maturity

I learned so much, I saw so much good and bad, through it all you were my provider and my security

Lord you customized my existence just for me. You were my shield. Thank you!!!

I looked and listened for you on yesterday

Written during my time with God, in a place of calm by
Dr. Cynthia Locke Henderson @ 5/3/2019

✎ God's word is powerful. What does this scripture say to you?

_____

_____

_____

_____

_____

✎ What have you learned during this time with Lord?

_____

_____

_____

_____

_____

✎ Are there things you need to do differently?

_____

_____

_____

_____

_____

✎ Before you leave this moment, write down God's directions to you.

_____

_____

_____

_____

_____

✎ Close this journaling moment with a prayer.

_____

_____

_____

_____

_____

Lord Forgive

————— ❦ —————

"So do not fear, for I am with you; be not dismayed, for I am your
God; I will strengthen you, I will help you, I will uphold you with my
righteous right hand."

(ISAIAH 41:10)

Lord there have been times when my motivation and strength are low
I did not feel like getting up or doing anything, I confess to you because
you already know
First, I must ask for your forgiveness because you NEVER get too tired
to give me your love and care
I can find you in many places, my lowliness, my mountain places and
even in my valley place you are there

Lord, you are my refuge and strength, I run to you when I have no one
that understands this state I am in
I want you to be my first choice in moments like this, I don't want any
other alternative that is a sin
I don't want to put tiredness before you, you have never done that to me
No matter what state I find myself in, Lord help me open the windows of
my heart and see only thee

Lord, thank you for forgiveness, it is my desire to ALWAYS honor and
worship you
You do give no prerequisite for blessing me, why should I have to give
excuses for the things I do
You love and forgive me unconditionally, your grace and your mercy
that seems to have no end
Thank you for making me your child, your daughter, your heir, and
making me your friend

Written during a time I did not feel like writing, but God made that feeling go away.
Dr. Cynthia Locke Henderson @ 5/6/2019

God's word is powerful. What does this scripture say to you?

_____
_____
_____
_____
_____

What have you learned during this time with Lord?

_____
_____
_____
_____
_____

Are there things you need to do differently?

_____
_____
_____
_____
_____

Before you leave this moment, write down God's directions to you.

_____
_____
_____
_____
_____

Close this journaling moment with a prayer.

_____
_____
_____
_____
_____

Lord You Repaired
My Broken Road

"I will open rivers on the bare heights and springs in the midst of the valleys; I will make the wilderness a pool of water and the dry land fountains of water"

(ISAIAH 41:18 NASB)

Lord, I accept your hand reaching for me to take me off this broken road
It seems I have been here spinning round and round until being here seems old
I have been wounded, scared and broken from the wear and tear of traveling this road from day to day
I feel thirsty from the dry areas and mentally low from the valley encounters along the way

There have been mountains that seem unclimbable and impassable, Lord they seemed too high
I know you have grown tired of my constantly asking why must I endure the broken place, Lord why
It was necessary for me to tunnel through mountains, to feel valley experiences, and to thirst for you
It was necessary to travel this road; it was not crowded but traveled by the chosen few

Your word reassures me that you can and will heal the broken hearted and bind the wounds from this trip
The things that I feel were taken, the things that I thought I needed you allowed me to skip

I trust your word that says you will restore health; the wounds are mere scars to remind me of the cause
As I reflect, I am overwhelmed by your grace and mercy, how can I do anything but take a thankful pause

Written during my time with God, in a place of calm
by Dr. Cynthia Locke Henderson @ 5/22/2019

God's word is powerful. What does this scripture say to you?

_____
_____
_____
_____
_____

What have you learned during this time with Lord?

_____
_____
_____
_____
_____

Are there things you need to do differently?

_____
_____
_____
_____
_____

Before you leave this moment, write down God's directions to you.

_____
_____
_____
_____
_____

Close this journaling moment with a prayer.

_____
_____
_____
_____
_____

You Give Strength Every Cycle

"…I am the LORD, who heals you."

(Exodus 15:26)

Lord, this life sends me in cycles of highs, middles and lows
One cycle, I trust you relentlessly and rest in the fact that you repair all
of my woes
I seem to go into valleys that seek to consume me with aloneness and
sense that I do not matter
My fight to trust you seems to falter and be strangely moved in a direction where trust scatters

Lord I have been in this middle space before
It seems to occur every time you give me an entrance into a high opened
door
Lord forgive me for not holding on to your word, as it is important as
the blood that runs through my veins
Your word is my light, my shield, my strength and the regulator of our
brains

Lord I wake this morning with you reminding me of your consistencies
and promises to see me as I am
Lord help me to focus on the power of your word to transform these
cycles and see you as God's lamb
You have purpose for me, you have shared your vision for me, you keep
moving me purposely forward
I am reminded that all of my life is in your hand and results come when
I call on the name of the LORD

This is the solution that the Lord game me to regulate my cycles on @6/3/2019,
Dr. Cynthia Locke Henderson

God's word is powerful. What does this scripture say to you?

_____

_____

_____

_____

_____

What have you learned during this time with Lord?

_____

_____

_____

_____

_____

Are there things you need to do differently?

_____

_____

_____

_____

_____

Before you leave this moment, write down God's directions to you.

_____

_____

_____

_____

_____

Close this journaling moment with a prayer.

_____

_____

_____

_____

_____

Lord I Thank You

Give thanks in all circumstances, for this is God's will
for you in Christ Jesus.

(1 Thessalonians 5:18)

Lord, you are always worthy of praise and glory
Without you in my life I would not be here to tell my story
As often as Satan has tried to take my life and stop your purpose in my life
As often as Satan has attempted to destroy by materializing others who
operated on strife

You, oh Lord, are my source and the author of my story and the drama in
my life's play
Some plots in my play seem to head in a different direction until you
Lord change the script to your way
Others thought they were MVP (Most Important Person) on the stage as
you groomed me for a certain role
You created my character, you implanted gifts and talents, you removed
the old and created in me a living soul

Lord, I sing praise silently in my heart and I write praise to you on paper,
on my computer and they are even in my thoughts
When I can't contain it all, I verbalize the highest praise to you,
"Hallelujah", thank you for connecting my dots
Thank you, Lord, for giving me a heart to love you and to desire to be all
that I can be for you
Thank you, Lord, for growing me, bringing me through trials of fire, and
walking with me on a road traveled by few

Lord you are my Alpha and you will be my Omega

Written as inspired by God alone on 6/4/2019, Dr. Cynthia Locke Henderson

God's word is powerful. What does this scripture say to you?

_____
_____
_____
_____
_____

What have you learned during this time with Lord?

_____
_____
_____
_____
_____

Are there things you need to do differently?

_____
_____
_____
_____
_____

Before you leave this moment, write down God's directions to you.

_____
_____
_____
_____

Close this journaling moment with a prayer.

_____
_____
_____
_____
_____

Oh, For Your Grace

Let us then approach God's throne of grace with confidence, so that we may receive mercy and find grace to help us in our time of need.

(HEBREWS 4:16)

You created us out of love and created a perfect world for us to dwell in
You gave us all that we needed and allowed us to freely live a life where
we had never been
You gave us instructions and you gave us choice
You talked with us in the garden and allowed us to hear your voice

It seems we continue with that mindset that enough is not enough
We are not always content with what you give and seek to get more stuff
You allow us to suffer from our own greedy needs for more to help us see
That you love us and want us to see, despite our imperfections you give
answers and solutions that are free

You are all knowing and aware of the sin on this earth
That is why you gave us your son through an immaculate birth
Still you made allowance for the sin that is so prevalent in our life race
You invite into repentance, give us mercy and still bless us from your
throne of GRACE

Thank you for grace that clears any sinful balance in my life and reminds
me that you always hear me.

God's word is powerful. What does this scripture say to you?

_____
_____
_____
_____
_____

What have you learned during this time with Lord?

_____
_____
_____
_____
_____

Are there things you need to do differently?

_____
_____
_____
_____
_____

Before you leave this moment, write down God's directions to you.

_____
_____
_____
_____
_____

Close this journaling moment with a prayer.

_____
_____
_____
_____
_____

I Am Entering Your Gates Lord

(Psalm 100:4. Psalm 119:130. Romans 8:26)

Lord, I enter your gates and leave the gates that have blocked within myself
I place my wants, worries and my cares in place that I can't change, I place them on this shelf
I enter thanking you that I even exist at this moment of surrendering
You see I wasted too much time seeking my own solutions instead of trusting what you are rendering

You direct us to give praise to you in everything whether life is moving in the direction I feel I need
Lord, I surrender all that is within this earthly temple, I move out of the way and let you take lead
You are so patient with the intricacies of me, you understand it all, from the complex to the private
I disassociate with those things that bring down and destroy me, those things that I made great

I did not create this body, I did not navigate my entry into this world, I am without creation credentials
Only you oh Lord continue to create in me potential, only you oh Lord give me life and the essentials
I thank you Lord for this moment of veracity, transparency, direction, purpose and mission significance
No matter the predicaments I get in, you let me know what it feels like and always arrive for my defense

Lord I miss my special time with you, just the two of us

God's word is powerful. What does this scripture say to you?

_____
_____
_____
_____
_____

What have you learned during this time with Lord?

_____
_____
_____
_____
_____

Are there things you need to do differently?

_____
_____
_____
_____
_____

Before you leave this moment, write down God's directions to you.

_____
_____
_____
_____
_____

Close this journaling moment with a prayer.

_____
_____
_____
_____
_____

Appreciativeness

I will bless the LORD at all times: his praise shall continually
be in my mouth.

(PSALM 34:1 KJV)

I lay down last night with gratitude for you and awoke this morning
with thankfulness
Realizing that my life had been blessed by you, when it could have
turned the other way and been a mess
I thank you as I realized the many dangers that were around me and
how close I was to death's door
Yet, you held death back, letting me know that you have work for me
and so much more

Lord, I repent for the times when I felt I was in charge and acted so
nonchalant and cavalier
There have been times I did not thank you for my existence, I just acted
like you are supposed to be near
There have been times when my behavior says to you "I got this", I know
what to do
Where would I be, who would I be, what would I be doing, who would I
be if it were not for you

Lord, I appreciate you being my Lord, my Savior, my shield and the
author to my story
Lord, I appreciate you Elohim for you are prominent, mighty and strong,
you are worthy of glory
You are Jehovah Rapha, that God that heals my body, my heart and my
emotions
Lord you are Jehovah Jireh; my provider who determines when I am due
promotions

Lord you are my "All and All". There is no replacement for you!

✏ God's word is powerful. What does this scripture say to you?

_____
_____
_____
_____
_____

✏ What have you learned during this time with Lord?

_____
_____
_____
_____
_____

✏ Are there things you need to do differently?

_____
_____
_____
_____
_____

✏ Before you leave this moment, write down God's directions to you.

_____
_____
_____
_____
_____

✏ Close this journaling moment with a prayer.

_____
_____
_____
_____
_____

Lord, I Can't Identify This Emptiness – Help!

The name of the LORD is a fortified tower;
the righteous run to it and are safe.

(PROVERBS 18:10)

Lord, please deliver me from myself and the emptiness that I now feel
I can't describe what I feel. It is not my body I really don't feel ill
I am in a space where I don't know what to pray, I don't know what
direction to go
I submit me to you, I submit this dullness, this feeling of uncertainty, I
really don't know

Lord, I am reminded that you have been there with me like a shadow
over my valley
When I have struggles to reach mountain tops your support has received
the highest tally
I have had dark clouds of life experiences, that seem to block my
sunshine event
I have had rains that fall in life creating a flood of emotions seemingly
everywhere I went

Then Lord you give me mornings like this where I come to you with
expectations that you will fix me
I come knowing you are my doctor, your word is the medicine that I
need, that I clearly see
You are my hiding place, my rock, my shield, my everything, my directions and my solution
The only thing you require of me is to trust you, and your word, you
manage my battles and retribution

Lord, you never let me down!

🖊 God's word is powerful. What does this scripture say to you?

_____
_____
_____
_____
_____

🖊 What have you learned during this time with Lord?

_____
_____
_____
_____
_____

🖊 Are there things you need to do differently?

_____
_____
_____
_____
_____

🖊 Before you leave this moment, write down God's directions to you.

_____
_____
_____
_____
_____

🖊 Close this journaling moment with a prayer.

_____
_____
_____
_____
_____

What Is Time That Thou Art Mindful Of

(PHILIPPIANS 4:8. ISAIAH 55:8-9)

We rush to get so many places and have no regards for what might happen in route
You bind the hand and actions of the enemy who would destroy us if you let him, there is no doubt
We give in to our exhaustion at the end of a day that you blessed us to have
You keep our heart pumping, blood flowing through it on time and not closing our heart's valve

Our thoughts take a momentary vacation away from thinking the way you said and living right in your sight
The Bible says think on these things, whatever is true, whatever is noble, whatever is right,
Additionally, the Bible says think on whatever is lovely, whatever is admirable and worthy of praise
You lead us because our thoughts are not yours and neither are our ways your ways

Lord, you control time, when it comes and where we go, how much of time we have to do the right thing
You give grace when we venture into wrong thoughts, you give mercy for the wrong things our actions bring
Lord help us to get it right, all the way right because you are not mindful to time, you are mindful of wrong
Help us not miss out. Thank you for making sure we have every chance to join you eternally on your throne

**Draw me close to your will and purpose for me in this life.
You're all I need!**

*Written during my time with the Lord and realizing the sacrifice He gives for me.
Dr. Cynthia Locke Henderson © June 20,2019*

God's word is powerful. What does this scripture say to you?

_____

_____

_____

_____

_____

What have you learned during this time with Lord?

_____

_____

_____

_____

_____

Are there things you need to do differently?

_____

_____

_____

_____

_____

Before you leave this moment, write down God's directions to you.

_____

_____

_____

_____

_____

Close this journaling moment with a prayer.

_____

_____

_____

_____

_____

Secret Place

PSALM 91:1

Lord, I am in the place where no one but you are allowed to be there
Only you can understand what I am feeling and understand the words of my silent prayer
Only you know the intricate corners where I wonder why things happen and where I store my tears
Our secret place has more space terabyte than my computer and holds memory from many years

Those secret feeling and thoughts sometimes invade my being and leaves me in a state of wondering
But when I get to the heart of my thoughts, I am compelled to see your face for all my questioning
I look at where you bought me from and how my experiences made me strong and touched countless souls
The rewards you have given when I have been obedient and the grace you give when I don't listen is never old

Lord, thank you for determining when merit is needed and for keeping our secrets between you and I
Thank you for valuing my tears in that place and giving reasons to all my questions asking why
Thank you for loving me in a way that no one has ever mastered or measured up too
Thank you for always being there when I need to feel you or hear from you in our secret place, just me and you

Lord, Thank You for Always Being There!

Written as inspired by God while in our secret place.
Dr. Cynthia Locke Henderson ©June 21,2019

✏ God's word is powerful. What does this scripture say to you?

_____

_____

_____

_____

✏ What have you learned during this time with Lord?

_____

_____

_____

_____

✏ Are there things you need to do differently?

_____

_____

_____

_____

✏ Before you leave this moment, write down God's directions to you.

_____

_____

_____

_____

✏ Close this journaling moment with a prayer.

_____

_____

_____

_____

_____

Forgiveness (My Rainbow Promise)

For if you forgive men their trespasses, your heavenly Father will also forgive you. But if you do not forgive men their trespasses, neither will your Father forgive your trespasses

(MATTHEW 6:14-15 NKJV)

After the floods in my life, God sent his symbol of covenant a rainbow
He touched my heart and allowed me to release and let the pains, hurts, scars of the past GO
Yes, they are there in my memory, but God has blessed how I recall
I no longer see the painful past as things that hold me down, whether they were great or small

Thank you, Lord, for allowing me to experience the power of forgiveness
No matter how far you may go, how much you may accomplish not forgiving makes all become less
You feel like you are moving forward, you are taking steps but not meeting GOD's requirements
Forgiveness is not a feeling, a sensation that makes things go away. It is a choice

The word of God unmistakably says we must forgive in order for God to forgive us
Whether you think a wrong or wicked thing has been done to you, forgiveness is a must
Sin does not discriminate and will attack anyone and especially those that call on the name of the Jesus

But God has sealed his covenant I will forgive you, if you forgive others. That promise is for all of us

Written in honor of forgiveness from God and my Rainbow Promise on ©June 23, 2019
by Dr. Cynthia Locke Henderson

God's word is powerful. What does this scripture say to you?

_____

_____

_____

_____

_____

What have you learned during this time with Lord?

_____

_____

_____

_____

_____

Are there things you need to do differently?

_____

_____

_____

_____

_____

Before you leave this moment, write down God's directions to you.

_____

_____

_____

_____

_____

Close this journaling moment with a prayer.

_____

_____

_____

_____

_____

Why Did It Take So Long?

(PSALM 8:28. JAMES 1:3)

Why did it take so long for my accuser to acknowledge the wrong done to me?
I often wondered if this person could simply be unaware of the intense pain and hurt, can't they feel and see
The path of their evil has run the span of many, many years
The repeated hurt, deceit, devastation has caused so many tears

The evil caused has rippled through a family destined for greatness
A family that pulled apart, then back together determined that we would be our best
Yes, it hurt, yes it disappointed, yes it scared, but NO it did not stop us
We felt all the impact, yet our faith and strength went from a negative to a mountain of plus

If we had known the significance of all things working together for good to those who love God, not man
If we had not understood that we were all called according to God's purpose and plan
Our trials tried our faith and developed perseverance and made us strong moms, sisters, and brothers
Testimonies and a living witness were demonstrated for us and for others

I am not so sure that my life would have gone the direction it did and would I be a witness to other mothers
There were many things to learn, many gifts that required maturity, growing a testimony that blessed others
I look back only to see how God kept me, molded me, graced me and

forgave me so that I could receive it back
I never gave up trusting God for preserving my soul and I never suffered lack

I thank God that acknowledgement did come and it came on God's timing and not mine
I thank God that my journey was rocking, scars formed, but God allowed me to progress and shine
God kept his promise and blessed my seed to have what it takes to win
My seed's seeds were blessed and my seeds continue to be blessed, Cornelius, Edward, Schnearia, Benjamin

All other ground is sinking sand!!!

✐ God's word is powerful. What does this scripture say to you?

_____
_____
_____
_____
_____

✐ What have you learned during this time with Lord?

_____
_____
_____
_____
_____

✐ Are there things you need to do differently?

_____
_____
_____
_____
_____

✐ Before you leave this moment, write down God's directions to you.

_____
_____
_____
_____
_____

✐ Close this journaling moment with a prayer.

_____
_____
_____
_____
_____

I Skipped My Time With You

"Have faith in God," Jesus answered.

(MARK 11:22)

Lord, too much time has passed since I took time to send you a written message
Yet you still love and forgive me without inflicting rage or turning your blessing page
I have missed the time we have together in the early mornings
Yet you have been faithfully watching over me and giving me warnings

You loved me when it felt like so much unlove was all around me
You did not allow anyone or anything, no not nothing, to disconnect the bond between me and thee
There have been so many inconsistencies in my life, so many broken promises, so many "let downs"
There have been so many things happening to me that could give me reason to frown

Lord, I am just a human with many unpredictable ways and wondering thoughts
I don't always take the time to thank you and give you time as I ought
Thank you for loving me and not giving up on me, not throwing in the towel or turning your back
Thanks for giving me a purposeful life and though I wander you bring me back to the track

Who would not serve a God like that?

Written to God as I was compelled by His faithfulness towards me and my loneliness without the time we spent "writing" on ©7/31/2019 by Dr. Cynthia Locke Henderson©

✎ God's word is powerful. What does this scripture say to you?

_____

_____

_____

_____

_____

✎ What have you learned during this time with Lord?

_____

_____

_____

_____

_____

✎ Are there things you need to do differently?

_____

_____

_____

_____

_____

✎ Before you leave this moment, write down God's directions to you.

_____

_____

_____

_____

_____

✎ Close this journaling moment with a prayer.

_____

_____

_____

_____

_____

My Timing Is Not Your Timing

The LORD is my light and my salvation – whom shall, I fear?
The LORD is the stronghold of my life – of whom shall I be afraid?

(PSALM 27:1)

Lord, sometimes I pray in desperation of a need, you know my needs and instantly come to my rescue
You know my heart and you know when I am in a place where I really don't know what I need to do
Sometimes my prayers are not overnight matters, yet I still pray them with limited expectations that you will do my task
Sometimes my prayers are for things that I really don't know if I am ready for them, or if I really want what I ask

I grow weary of waiting for a response to some prayers and resign my thoughts to thinking that prayer is not for me
I vacillate from wanting, not waiting, not trusting, not having faith, not expecting, and sometimes forgetting my plea
How that must feel Lord, when I so quickly forget the times that you replied to my requests at just the right time
Lord, please forgive me for every time that I measure your time with mine, that is simply not right and is a faith crime

You have put up with my inconsistences for many years because you alone know what I need and when I need it
You know what giving me everything I want will do, when you already know the plans you have for me and its intent
Lord, help me to trust that you will unwaveringly answer my NEEDS and to have great expectations in your customized plan
Your plan does not need manipulation, you predestined me, my life is directed by you, all I need you will do and can

Lord I pray with great expectations that you will take charge!

Written during my time with Lord and realizing that I am not praying with full expectation by Dr. Cynthia Locke Henderson on 8/5/2018©

✏ God's word is powerful. What does this scripture say to you?

_____

_____

_____

_____

_____

✏ What have you learned during this time with Lord?

_____

_____

_____

_____

_____

✏ Are there things you need to do differently?

_____

_____

_____

_____

_____

✏ Before you leave this moment, write down God's directions to you.

_____

_____

_____

_____

_____

✏ Close this journaling moment with a prayer.

_____

_____

_____

_____

_____

Lord My Hands Write What My Heart Speaks

Some trust in chariots and some in horses,
but we trust in the name of the LORD our GOD.

(PSALM 20:7)

There are many thoughts and feelings collaborated between my mind and heart
One fact is constant in the collaboration is that you love me and you have the main part
Indecisiveness attacks my desire for commitment to trusting you completely
You allow me to try things on my own, fall, fail, then you restore so sweetly

Even now I fear to ask you not to not let me be alone on the earth
Does my aloneness deserve another's worth?
Is it fair to keep this collaboration between my mind and heart and now my feelings?
Lord you have brought me from a mighty long way, but this collaboration questions my complete healing?

I look back to see the many treasures you have given to me, the love that has never stopped
I look back and see you have not left me, I am in your heart, you have not allowed my name to be dropped
When I think you are not listening to the collaboration you send me a sign letting me now you are there
There is nowhere on this earth that my mind and heart forget that you are EVERY WHERE!!

Written as only God could inspire me at a time when I did not know what to pray.
Dr. Cynthia L. Henderson 8/19/2019©

God's word is powerful. What does this scripture say to you?

_____

_____

_____

_____

_____

What have you learned during this time with Lord?

_____

_____

_____

_____

_____

Are there things you need to do differently?

_____

_____

_____

_____

_____

Before you leave this moment, write down God's directions to you.

_____

_____

_____

_____

_____

Close this journaling moment with a prayer.

_____

_____

_____

_____

_____

What Is Blocking The Door?

Here I am! I stand at the door and knock. If anyone hears my voice
and opens the door, I will come in and eat with that person,
and they with me.

(REVELATION 3:20)

I know it is time to move clutters of fear and not knowing the unknown
You would think, after all you have brought me through that by now, I
would have grown
You literally saved my life, you allowed me to learn so much when I
thought I was not teachable
Lord, your voice saturates my environment on my mountains and in my
valleys that seem reachable

In Psalm 32:8 you promised to teach me in the way I need to go and to
use your eyes for my vision
I know you will because you have fixed my brokenness and errors with
precision
You have dried my tears and lifted my soul so many times in so many
intricate ways
You have multiplied resources that seem to expire in seconds and
extended your blessings for days

Lord, at this moment it is difficult for me to imagine the exhilaration of
having a true mate
I have identified that blockage as fear of the past causing me this
tremendous weight
I surrender knowing that you hold my right hand, saying "fear not" I
will help you
With faith the size of a mustard seed, I surrender asking you to do what
you need to do

The LORD himself goes before you and will be with you; he will never leave you nor forsake you. Do not be afraid; do not be discouraged."
(Deuteronomy 31:8)

How can I not serve a God who speaks to me through his word at the right time every time?

Written while the Lord spoke directly to me and every one of my fears.
Dr. Cynthia Locke Henderson 8/20/2019©

God's word is powerful. What does this scripture say to you?

_____
_____
_____
_____
_____

What have you learned during this time with Lord?

_____
_____
_____
_____
_____

Are there things you need to do differently?

_____
_____
_____
_____
_____

Before you leave this moment, write down God's directions to you.

_____
_____
_____
_____
_____

Close this journaling moment with a prayer.

_____
_____
_____
_____
_____

Take A Bird's Point Of View

Look at the birds of the air; they do not sow or reap or store away in barns, and yet your heavenly Father feeds them. Are you not much more valuable than they?

(MATTHEW 6:26)

Whatever you are holding on to, let go and trust the master's hand
for the rest of your trip
As you hold on to it nothing comes in nor goes out because of your grip
When we met last, your door was not opened because of obstruction
and blockage
Trusting in me seemed a concept very difficult for you to gauge

Let's take a different perspective because I will not give up on you
No matter how distracted, how aloof, how detached you are in the many
purposeless things you do
Won't you realize you are my child, my chosen one, I know your name
I have never left you; I will not forsake you; I have purpose for you, I am
your father I am still the same

The birds in the air awaken and take flight every day without a care
They travel without packing a meal because they know I am everywhere
They don't worry about tomorrow; they trust the strength and affection I
give and my direction
They fly forward with no worry of what's ahead or what's left behind,
they rest in my protection

**If I care for the birds of the air, how much more valuable
are you to me!**

*Written as I found my way back to my private time with the Lord. He was waiting to tell
me how much he cared on ©9/23/2019. Dr. Cynthia Locke Henderson*

God's word is powerful. What does this scripture say to you?

_____

_____

_____

_____

_____

What have you learned during this time with Lord?

_____

_____

_____

_____

_____

Are there things you need to do differently?

_____

_____

_____

_____

_____

Before you leave this moment, write down God's directions to you.

_____

_____

_____

_____

Close this journaling moment with a prayer.

_____

_____

_____

_____

_____

Focus

———— ❦ ————

Let us then approach God's throne of grace with confidence, so that we may receive mercy and find grace to help us in our time of need.

(HEBREWS 4:16)

Our eyes are the windows which we see the things we face day after day
They see some things that bring floods flowing down our face in an uncontrollable way
They see things that cause us to take focus off of the Lord, it is him who controls all
The Lord wants us to shift our focus, not on what we see but, on his call
The space between what we see is often clouded by our desire to make changes as we see
When sometimes things are there for us to contact the Lord and just let it be
We don't have to try to fix everything, we have to leave it to God because he sees it too
Take what you see before the Lord and seek his wisdom on what to do

God made these intricate bodies that we have and he is the master regulator
He is a problem solver, he is light in tunnel vision, he is the fixer of my vision and so much more
He will bring focus if I just ask Him what should I do, what should I think, what should I say
He replies in a heartbeat, he does not waver unless wait time is needed, He does it his way

Written as INSPIRED by God during our journaling time alone. An intimate answer to help me focus on ©9/24/2019, Dr. Cynthia Locke Henderson

God's word is powerful. What does this scripture say to you?

_____

_____

_____

_____

_____

What have you learned during this time with Lord?

_____

_____

_____

_____

_____

Are there things you need to do differently?

_____

_____

_____

_____

_____

Before you leave this moment, write down God's directions to you.

_____

_____

_____

_____

_____

Close this journaling moment with a prayer.

_____

_____

_____

_____

_____

Healing Is Needed

The LORD is close to the brokenhearted and
saves those who are crushed in spirit.

(PSALM 34:18)

Oh Lord, my king, my healer, my source, my peace, my provider, my
strength through it all
You are the lifter of my head, the heart regulator, the only one there
when I fall
You are the solutions when I don't know where to turn, when to be still
and know that you are God
You are the one that reaches out to me when I am drowning in despair
and think I am flawed

I am who I am supposed to be, help me accept that and rejoice in your
decision to create me
My life is predestined, my steps are ordered by you and not in the direction I think they should be
I wake every day to your invitation to enter the dawning of a new day
and a new assignment
I wake for your healing of scars and memories not needed as you master
my refinement

Healing is needed in this body that has been tattered and torn, broken
from inside out
Healing is needed is for the pain caused by life's impact to make me doubt
Healing is needed as I lose myself and yield myself more to you Lord
and what I should do
Healing is needed as I shift my desire to following your directions
having faith in YOU

*Written as God spoke direction into my life and healing to my soul on 9/25/19 during our
special time together. ©Dr. Cynthia Locke Henderson*

*) God's word is powerful. What does this scripture say to you?

_____

_____

_____

_____

_____

*) What have you learned during this time with Lord?

_____

_____

_____

_____

_____

*) Are there things you need to do differently?

_____

_____

_____

_____

_____

*) Before you leave this moment, write down God's directions to you.

_____

_____

_____

_____

_____

*) Close this journaling moment with a prayer.

_____

_____

_____

_____

_____

Danger All Around

—— ❦ ——

Peace I leave with you; my peace I give you. I do not give to you as the
world gives. Do not let your hearts be troubled and do not be afraid

(JOHN 14:27)

Lord, thank you for truly protecting me every day, every hour, every
minute, down to the second
You keep your eyes on me inside my body and outside, that is your
commitment to our unbreakable bond
How lightly we take your blessings and commitment to give and leave
peace with us around the clock

As I lay down at night, I sleep under the protection of a lock that could
be broken in late in the dark
Accidents do not discriminate, they can occur anytime, anywhere when
you think you are alone
I do realize that you look out for me when I come and when I go, you
watch me from your throne
My heart was created by you, it could stop at any time or become in
danger because of illness
However, it is during this time that I take peace knowing that you regulate my mind and heart in my stillness

You are my shield, my strength, my mercy, my keeper, my watchman,
Jehovah Shalom, my peace
It does not matter where I am nor what I am doing, whether I am in the
north, south, west or east
I am because you are, I am where I am because you predestine me to be,
I am who I am because of you
Lord thank you for keeping me in your hand and heart, thank you that
no matter what I am in your view

Do not be anxious about anything, but in every situation, by prayer and petition, with thanksgiving, present your requests to God.
(Philippians 4:6)

Lord, you've got me coming and going. Thank You

✎ God's word is powerful. What does this scripture say to you?

_____

_____

_____

_____

_____

✎ What have you learned during this time with Lord?

_____

_____

_____

_____

_____

✎ Are there things you need to do differently?

_____

_____

_____

_____

_____

✎ Before you leave this moment, write down God's directions to you.

_____

_____

_____

_____

_____

✎ Close this journaling moment with a prayer.

_____

_____

_____

_____

_____

On My Way To Here

————— ❧ ~❧❧ —————

But if from there you seek the LORD your God, you will find him
if you seek him with all your heart and with all your soul.

(DEUTERONOMY 4:29)

Lord, what a complex trip to get here somethings were supposed to
happen and somethings were a miss
Efforts were made to stop my journey, but Lord you saved me for such a
time as this
You saved me from being tossed in a river with my mom, my brother
You sent an angel to rescue when there was no hope to struggle any
more, there was no other

You put death on an assignment to leave my mother, my brother, and I alone
You sent an angel that stayed making sure that all hopelessness was gone
You put a determination in our mom that refused to give in to poverty,
ignorance, and defeat
Our mom passed it on to us and others, what a priceless gift that I
continue to pass without missing a beat

Now Lord as time has passed, I find myself here where you ordained me
to live and survive
You sent tests to help me grow, and realize that what you gave my mom
has helped me thrive
People came in my life to hurt, to love, to add, to subtract, to multiply
and attempt to take your space
Lord, it has been a purposeful journey to get here, please control my life
and not let it be a waste

*"I am the vine; you are the branches. If you remain in me and I in you,
you will bear much fruit; apart from me you can do nothing" (John 15:5)*

I came to devotion feeling empty and this is what the Lord gave me on 9/27/19
© *Dr. Cynthia Locke Henderson*

God's word is powerful. What does this scripture say to you?

_____

_____

_____

_____

What have you learned during this time with Lord?

_____

_____

_____

_____

Are there things you need to do differently?

_____

_____

_____

_____

Before you leave this moment, write down God's directions to you.

_____

_____

_____

_____

Close this journaling moment with a prayer.

_____

_____

_____

_____

_____

God Has Your Answers, Listen As His Words Speak

If my people, who are called by my name, will humble themselves and pray and seek my face and turn from their wicked ways, then I will hear from heaven, and I will forgive their sin and will heal their land.

(II Chronicles 7:14)

God is constantly talking to us as we pray, as we cry, as our goes hurt so deep
We are noisy with discomfort, worrying, complaining, and tremendous anxiety that we can't sleep
We are not aware that God is listening and wants to give us instruction in what we need to know
We have endured a lot, but the battle is not ours to fight, more test and trials are ahead if we want to grow

This is not the time to have an argument against God for what is upsetting life
This is not the time that we give into the forces around us with all of envy and strife
This is the time when we listen and know that we wage war against principalities and darkness in the earth
We don't war against flesh and blood; we ask and receive mercy and grace from God who knows our worth

So "hush" and listen as he speaks to heart, responding to our pleas and directing our struggles and despair
Replace every word of pain with a call on the name of Jesus, he is everywhere listening to our prayer

There is power in his name, demons run, because Jesus has the authority to break every chain

All other names you call are sinking sand, "hush" and listen, in him you will always gain

Finally, be strong in the Lord and in his mighty power. (Ephesians 6:10)

Inspired as I listen to God used my daughter to speak before she sang the song "Rescue".
This is what God gave on © 9/30/2019 Dr. Cynthia Locke Henderson

God's word is powerful. What does this scripture say to you?

_____
_____
_____
_____
_____

What have you learned during this time with Lord?

_____
_____
_____
_____
_____

Are there things you need to do differently?

_____
_____
_____
_____
_____

Before you leave this moment, write down God's directions to you.

_____
_____
_____
_____
_____

Close this journaling moment with a prayer.

_____
_____
_____
_____
_____
_____

You Blessed My Seeds

Remain in me, as I also remain in you. No branch can bear
fruit by itself; it must remain in the vine. Neither can you
bear fruit unless you remain in me.

(JOHN 15:4)

Lord, I petition you on behalf of my seeds and ask for your continued
protection around them
Efforts seem to taunt them and tries desperately to discourage them and
pull them from your realm
You have kept your promise and allowed them to excel beyond man's
imagination
You continue to bring them through and out of complex situations without a spirit of retaliation

I thank you for my seed, the multi-tiered gifts and talent you have steered
others to invest
Man cannot phantom their worth, however, man is aware that they
continue to stand against all test
You have allowed them to rise on wings of eagles, soaring through life's
adversities and poverties
They traveled roads lined with heart wrenching pain unseen by others
who only see their ease

Lord, they are my seed, I feel their pain and pray for your lead to their
next chapters, new missions
I trust you to bring them to the top, you have always done, and prepare
them for transitions
More than anything else I continue to pray that they do not lose sight
and heart of your love

I pray they realize nothing on earth takes credit for the benefits of their life, it comes from you above

Lord, I continue to surrender their care to you, take charge.

Written during my silent prayer and conversation with the Lord on the behalf of my seed
©10/1/19, by Dr. Cynthia Locke Henderson

God's word is powerful. What does this scripture say to you?

_____

_____

_____

_____

_____

What have you learned during this time with Lord?

_____

_____

_____

_____

_____

Are there things you need to do differently?

_____

_____

_____

_____

_____

Before you leave this moment, write down God's directions to you.

_____

_____

_____

_____

_____

Close this journaling moment with a prayer.

_____

_____

_____

_____

_____

Thank You For An Upgrade

Do not be anxious about anything, but in every situation, by prayer
and petition, with thanksgiving, present your requests to God.

(PHILIPPIANS 4:6)

Lord, I have wasted so much time anxiously trying to figure things
out on my own
I have wasted time lingering over things that seem to always go wrong
I have wasted time in my worship with the impact of things done to
destroy me and discount me
I have simply wasted time thinking instead of praying, being noisy with
complaints and things I can't see

Lord, there is no reason why I should find myself in this same spot over
and over again
There is no reason that my focus should be off of you, I really need to
stay in my lane
You promised to be my protector and you have not wavered, I have not
suffered lack, you have trusted me
It is time for me to trust you for the Holy Spirit that you sent to keep me,
you have heard my plea

Thank you for reminding me that I am due for an upgrade and all I need
is to make my request known
You did not create me to be overwhelmed with anxiousness, and doubt
so now in your wisdom I have grown
You have not given me a spirit of fear, you give me love continually and
you give me power
The world has changed, you are the same. You change me as needed; you
have upgraded me for this hour

Even to your old age and gray hairs I am he, I am he who will sustain
you. I have made you and I will carry you; I will sustain you and
I will rescue you (Isaiah 46:4)

God's word is powerful. What does this scripture say to you?

_____

_____

_____

_____

_____

What have you learned during this time with Lord?

_____

_____

_____

_____

_____

Are there things you need to do differently?

_____

_____

_____

_____

_____

Before you leave this moment, write down God's directions to you.

_____

_____

_____

_____

_____

Close this journaling moment with a prayer.

_____

_____

_____

_____

_____

_____

It Is Another Day, And The Lord Has Kept Me

Behold, I am the LORD, the God of all flesh.
Is anything too hard for me?

(JEREMIAH 32:27 KJV)

Lord, I allowed others to frustrate and humiliate me to a point of
anger and failure to consult you
It seemed I had held so many emotions down until I allowed others to
simply unscrew
Please forgive me for giving away the power that you gave me that is
above all other power
There is power in your name, yes there is power to let you control the
situation during every hour

Anger is a natural part of our feelings, but it becomes unnatural when we
allow others to control
It is no good when it impacts the thoughts of our mind and threatens
contamination to our soul
Lord, please help me believe that you can control anger, all things are
possible when I believe
You constructed me to not allow anger to take away peace and make me
want to roll up my sleeves

When I allow anger to take a seat in my emotions, my thoughts, my way
my moments to reason
You have cautioned me to not grow weary in well doings, because you
will bless in due season

You see what I am up against and you see the scheming, tricks, hatred channeled at me you see it all

You give me time to fall, but you are always there if I just have faith and take the time to call

I did not need much, all I needed was a "mustard seed" moment

Written as God talked to me about my anger and need to take a mustard seed moment on 10/3/19 © Dr. Cynthia Locke Henderson

📝 God's word is powerful. What does this scripture say to you?

_____
_____
_____
_____
_____

📝 What have you learned during this time with Lord?

_____
_____
_____
_____
_____

📝 Are there things you need to do differently?

_____
_____
_____
_____
_____

📝 Before you leave this moment, write down God's directions to you.

_____
_____
_____
_____
_____

📝 Close this journaling moment with a prayer.

_____
_____
_____
_____
_____

I Have Purpose

You make known to me the path of life; you will fill me with joy in
your presence, with eternal pleasures at your right hand.

(PSALM 16:11)

Lord, thank you for purpose in my time here on this earth
I did not always know why you allowed me to be born, I did not always
know my worth
This baby girl who grew to become a woman went through much to get
here where I find myself today
I came through happy times, sick times, abusive times, testing times,
trying to do things my way

I know that I was not born because Thelma needed a little girl or a
second child
There were times life demanded a lot for our survival, but other times I
was the reason you gave her a smile
There were reasons that you selected her to be my mom, she was part of
the purpose you had for me
Living under her guidance impacted how I saw the world, but more
important, how I could see thee

You planted so many gifts and lessons in me to be shared with others, to
give reasons for living to others
You used my mom to nurture and inspire my purpose and made room
for it with my sisters and brothers
With a simple pencil and paper next to my bed where I could write to
and for you when moments were scary
You knew my story, the path I would travel, you met in my sleep and
awakening hour giving me vocabulary

You gave me power to write, power, peace, healing, struggles, deliverance, wisdom, direction, survival, and purpose starting with one pencil and a piece of paper. My purpose began so long ago, Thanks for letting me keep it for so long

Lord, from the heavens to the earth you created it all
You gave life where there was desolation and gave me family some short like me and some tall
You gave me sons that would grow to honor me as a queen, mother and friend
We would go our separate ways but never disconnect or sever the line of our family in the end

You gave me daughters, my ladies of wisdom, wit, intelligence, loveliness giving their best
They carried my granddaughters - Sierra, Simon, Nina, Sunshine all medical miracles surviving the test
The you gave me grandsons - Elijah and Adonis handsome and 100% all boys
They would secure a place in my heart that could not be replaced with any created toys

I love them all for they gave me the desire to remain in this place called earth
For a long time, it was my desire to never allow them to suffer lack from the time of their birth
Things, people, friends, places were taken away from me, you made us strong in the face of calamity
You gave me family, we went through the bad turned to good, after all was said and done, we are family

Written during my time with God and reflecting on his blessing of family that began with Cornelius, Edward, Schnearia, Benjamin and Suzanna on 10/5/19
© Dr. Cynthia Locke Henderson

_/_ God's word is powerful. What does this scripture say to you?

_____

_____

_____

_____

_____

_/_ What have you learned during this time with Lord?

_____

_____

_____

_____

_/_ Are there things you need to do differently?

_____

_____

_____

_____

_/_ Before you leave this moment, write down God's directions to you.

_____

_____

_____

_____

_/_ Close this journaling moment with a prayer.

_____

_____

_____

_____

_____

Modify And Move Forward

The sacrifice you desire is a broken spirit. You will not reject
a broken and repentant heart, O God

(Psalm 51:17 NLT)

Lord, New Vision Church has been broken so that we can re-access
who we are and whose we are
You have revealed thoughts, interpretation, feelings that were clogging
our feeling and revealing our scar
Souls in pain with thoughts tearing us apart when in fact it was helping
us move towards repentance
We needed to present ourselves as living sacrifices, desiring to be better,
desiring for another chance

To reach a contemporary world, to feel empty spaces, to shift the trend of
what we were facing
You brought us to a halt, exposed secrets that were deep within and
changed dreams that we were chasing
We had to modify to a transformation and renewing of our mind to seek
the perfect will of God
The pain we jointly felt, the tears we shed, the relationships broken, the
need for repenting was hard

We are here in a place where we must hear God, no matter how simple or
complex the directions
We have to modify and move forward trusting that God did not bring us
this far without corrections
This world has evolved over time, technology has changed, old habits,
ways and thoughts must fade
Because New Vision we must surrender "all" and make preparation, for
it's time for our upgrade

Jesus is the only one that has not changed. He remains the same, yesterday, today and forever more!

Written as I felt the heart of my church and sought God for uplifting words 10/17/2019
@ Dr. Cynthia Locke Henderson

✎ God's word is powerful. What does this scripture say to you?

_____
_____
_____
_____
_____

✎ What have you learned during this time with Lord?

_____
_____
_____
_____
_____

✎ Are there things you need to do differently?

_____
_____
_____
_____
_____

✎ Before you leave this moment, write down God's directions to you.

_____
_____
_____
_____
_____

✎ Close this journaling moment with a prayer.

_____
_____
_____
_____
_____

The Answer

I will bless the LORD at all times: his praise
shall continually be in my mouth.

(Psalm 34:1 KJV)

Lord, thank you for the benefit of thanksgiving and praise no matter
what
Thank you for being able to look the enemy face to face to be able to
keep my lips shut
Only you know the warfare that is going on within my heart
Only you have the solution that I need to keep standing in the midst of
confusion and keeping me set apart

Lord, I yield all that is within me to bless your name because that is my
source of power
Only you can calm the rage, dissipate the anger and change me for that hour
Instead of using my astuteness to challenge and engage in a battle that is
not mine
I hear your **answer** to call on the name of Jesus for that makes everything just fine

You, Lord, are worthy of my praise even when the situation seems far
above what I can master
Lord, you are my strong tower, my strength, you are my answer no
matter the disaster
You, Lord, are my salvation and my solution to all that life sends my
way; all I need is you
When I have no direction, I don't know what to do, you are my **answer**
you know what I need to do

Can't He do it? Won't He do it? Yes, He can. He is the Answer

*Written during a time when I needed to acknowledge that somethings are not for me to
figure out. Jesus is my answer on 10/8/3019 @ Dr. Cynthia Locke Henderson*

God's word is powerful. What does this scripture say to you?

_____

_____

_____

_____

_____

What have you learned during this time with Lord?

_____

_____

_____

_____

_____

Are there things you need to do differently?

_____

_____

_____

_____

_____

Before you leave this moment, write down God's directions to you.

_____

_____

_____

_____

_____

Close this journaling moment with a prayer.

_____

_____

_____

_____

_____

_____

You Had To Do It And I Am Glad

For I know the plans I have for you," declares the LORD,
"plans to prosper you and not to harm you,
plans to give you hope and a future.

(JEREMIAH 29:11)

I find it difficult to say He did not have to do it but He did, God completes his plans
He had me in His plan before this world was formed, every tissue, body organ and glands
I was part of his plan, so it is that, I choose to focus on in this human form
Thank God that I was part of his bigger plan and that my life mattered not according to man's norm

He gave me tears that dropped when I felt pain that you can see and pain unseen
Everything in my life would not always be perfect and only God knows what that would mean
He gave me a heart of determination that continued to pump life in me to weather the storms
Those storms came hard, tore me apart emotionally, but God gave victory no matter the forms

There were times that I wanted to give up and cease to exist, that was not in my control
God gave me what was needed to go through despite the adversity because he held my soul

God allowed me to have lows, so I would know the difference when He elevated me to a high

God has promised to never leave nor forsake me; so, when test comes my way, I don't have to say why

My flesh and my heart may fail, but God is the strength of my heart and my portion forever. (Psalm 73:26)

✎ God's word is powerful. What does this scripture say to you?

_____
_____
_____
_____
_____

✎ What have you learned during this time with Lord?

_____
_____
_____
_____
_____

✎ Are there things you need to do differently?

_____
_____
_____
_____
_____

✎ Before you leave this moment, write down God's directions to you.

_____
_____
_____
_____
_____

✎ Close this journaling moment with a prayer.

_____
_____
_____
_____
_____

Victory When Unfairness Isn't Fair

Trust in the LORD with all your heart and lean not
on your own understanding.

(Proverbs 3:5)

Lord, it is hard to accept unfairness because we are trying to prove
unfairness is not fair
Coupled with feelings that no one really understands and that they don't
even care
When you have given what seems like your all
When it seems like you have been designated to take the fall

You finally realized that unfairness will never ever be fair, but always a
divergent
Making you feel that others need to feel and see what you see is urgent
Lord thank you for helping me see that in the mist of complex unfairness you are in control
You allowed me to see beyond what's in my immediate vision, I must
cease striving to get my story told

You are always my rescue and allowing all things to work together for
good of those that trust you
Lord, I thank you for cultivating fairness in the middle of strife, racism,
hurtfulness, and a conniving peruse
Lord, thank you for letting me know that my situation was not hidden
from you, you were there
Thou I felt defenseless and like I was losing a battle you gave me victory
and removed the scare

*And we know that in all things God works for the good of those who love
him, who have been called according to his purpose (Romans 8:28)*

God's word is powerful. What does this scripture say to you?

_____
_____
_____
_____
_____

What have you learned during this time with Lord?

_____
_____
_____
_____
_____

Are there things you need to do differently?

_____
_____
_____
_____
_____

Before you leave this moment, write down God's directions to you.

_____
_____
_____
_____
_____

Close this journaling moment with a prayer.

_____
_____
_____
_____
_____

Lord, Thank You For Remembering The Good

You will keep in perfect peace those whose minds are steadfast,
because they trust in you.

(ISAIAH 26:3)

My earliest memory is on an Easter Day, dressed in a yellow, white,
and blue dress
I remember mom pressed my hair, bought brand new shoes, pretty socks
and made me look my best
I remember having such great difficulty breathing, I had asthma just like
my mom
So many nights I went to sleep with her rubbing my chest with healing
oil and holding me in her arm

But on this special Easter Day, she took me for prayer at Sis. Gilmore's
house and requested prayer
When I, a little girl walked in her house I felt a special presence in her
house everywhere
She began speaking in tongues and anointing me especially in my chest
as I struggle to breathe
When she finished everyone began thanking you Lord, for after that day,
I breathed with ease

I remember my nose bleeding profusely, no reason that I knew, my mom
prayed and kept wiping blood up
I remember an old remedy putting brown paper under my upper lip and
mom giving prayer of water in a cup

Soon the rag she was using to wipe my nose changed and only rung out clear water, bleeding stopped
Mom brought her prayer to a stop with Thank you Lord. The brown paper under my lip was dropped

I remember a desire to be tall enough to reach the sink so that I could wash the pots, utensils, and plates
Everyone took their chance to wash dishes my week was ending and I could hardly wait
So, I stood on an old metal can that I used as a stool to help me reach the sink, and not get all wet
I had matured to a level never experienced by people short like me, the dishes were cleaner I bet

As I found consolation in being tall only for a moment, a whistling sound went over my head just as I finished
That whistling sound came from a bullet fired to where I stood, my desire to be tall quickly diminished
This time I realized that if I was taller, my life would have ended there, but God was not finished with me
This was another one of those times that mom prayed and I did too, whatever you have for me Lord let it be

I remember feeling like Adam and Eve in the garden of Eden with all sorts of treasures, water flowing free
I knew where the best blackberries grew, a field of plum bushes, and climbing experiences up in a tree
Bushes and flowers around me, rinsing my feet in the streams; I remember not being afraid to be alone
I trusted that the Jesus I heard about in Sunday School was looking down on me from his throne

Now 67 about to be 68 and I can still feel mom's prayers over me, Lord
Thank you for letting her be who you wanted her to be
I am without mom, but the power and benefits of her prayers are things that I have grown to feel and see

Miracles in my life have multiplied, blessings continue, and the prayers have not stopped that's how we talk

Lord as my life continues please help how I remember, how I pray and steady me as I continue to walk.

Peace I leave with you; my peace I give you. I do not give to you as the world gives. Do not let your hearts be troubled and do not be afraid.
(John 14:27)

Written as inspired by God as he allowed me remember the power of prayer over my life and in my life. 10/10/1019 @ Dr. Cynthia Locke Henderson

✏️ God's word is powerful. What does this scripture say to you?

_____
_____
_____
_____
_____

✏️ What have you learned during this time with Lord?

_____
_____
_____
_____
_____

✏️ Are there things you need to do differently?

_____
_____
_____
_____
_____

✏️ Before you leave this moment, write down God's directions to you.

_____
_____
_____
_____
_____

✏️ Close this journaling moment with a prayer.

_____
_____
_____
_____
_____

Light My Way, You See What I Can't See

Your word is a lamp for my feet, a light on my path.

(PSALM 119:105)

Lord, thank you for all of the parts that you manage and play in my life's agenda
You speak to my heart with loving care and concerns, your words you send tenderly
Your word is a lamp for my feet in a very dark, vindictive, malicious territory
In the midst of all that goes on around me you always give me a victorious story

I don't know what each day will bring my way, what trials will make me strong
Or what things come as lambs, when they are wolves with motives that's wrong
Your word is instruction about how I should respond no matter the impact or insult
Lord, please help me to rely on instructions and not migrating to a failing rut

Lord, this day you gave to me, help me to represent you in all that comes my way
I am your child, your ambassador, your peace maker, your soldier for this day
I have your word and all that you predestined for this part of my existence

Lord I am not, will not give up, I am your heir and plan to go the distance

...so is my word that goes out from my mouth: It will not return to me empty, but will accomplish what I desire and achieve the purpose for which I sent it (Isaiah 55:11).

God's word is powerful. What does this scripture say to you?

_____

_____

_____

_____

_____

What have you learned during this time with Lord?

_____

_____

_____

_____

_____

Are there things you need to do differently?

_____

_____

_____

_____

_____

Before you leave this moment, write down God's directions to you.

_____

_____

_____

_____

_____

Close this journaling moment with a prayer.

_____

_____

_____

_____

_____

Broken To Be Made Whole

But the Lord is with me like a mighty warrior;
so my persecutors will stumble and not prevail.
They will fail and be thoroughly disgraced;
their dishonor will never be forgotten

(JEREMIAH 20:11)

I find myself being reminded that you had me in your thoughts before I
came, your view was a wider scope
You loved me and you know my name, you have plans for my future
wrapped up with hope
Some say I was the result of an illegitimate birth by a father who don't
know me and I don't know him
Man would have painted my life and project to be quite grim with no
vision and very dim

Lord, I've gone through a breaking and continue being broken so that
you make me better
Lord, I view your breaking as shaping and fixing things to help me
through the storm and all types weather
No science, no genealogy can determine my beginning no anthropology
can determine my behavior
To have gone through life threatening events, racism, hatred, abuse, yet I
stand because of my Savior

I don't always like the breaking process; however, I know that I am
mended, restored, and stronger
Each time you recondition me so that I stand still, I can see you working, my endurance is much longer
Because I know who I am and whose I am, I know you fix the broken
pieces with tenacity firmer than gold

My soul is in your hands, my repair is by the master craftsman who knows what it takes to make me whole

Written with direct inspiration from God who reminded me of a song I frequently sang, "Because He Lives" on 10/16/19 @ Dr. Cynthia Locke Henderson

🖊 God's word is powerful. What does this scripture say to you?

_____

_____

_____

_____

_____

🖊 What have you learned during this time with Lord?

_____

_____

_____

_____

_____

🖊 Are there things you need to do differently?

_____

_____

_____

_____

_____

🖊 Before you leave this moment, write down God's directions to you.

_____

_____

_____

_____

_____

🖊 Close this journaling moment with a prayer.

_____

_____

_____

_____

_____

_____

Many Things Die Lord, But You Refused To Die Permanently

We are hard pressed on every side, but not crushed; perplexed, but not in despair; persecuted, but not abandoned; struck down, but not destroyed.

(II CORINTHIANS 4:8,9)

Lord, thank you because you gave your life for me to live
Yet you came back with all power and victory that no man can give
I can see that concept in many things around me to remind me of your endured shame
Unlike so many other things and people you saw my sinful life and you came

Leaves turn colors, fall to the earth and die, the tree becomes empty protected only by the bark
It stands uncovered, yet in the spring you give it renewed beauty that accentuate its brokenness and marks
The tree stands for a season shameless because it knows rejuvenation is coming in the spring
We too are scared from the guilt, shame, hurts, failures. Because you refused to die, redemption is what you bring

I have to let many things go in the fall seasons of my life because they are no longer useful for my growth
I suffer the loss of many things during my down season, however, I have learned to stand still because of your oath

You promised to love me despite my imperfection, my perplexity, my despair, my pressures, my abandonment
You said you would rise again, you refused to die, you rose again for me in my past and are stronger in my present

Written with inspiration of God's promise to me, I am never without his love on
10/17/2019 @ Dr. Cynthia Locke Henderson

God's word is powerful. What does this scripture say to you?

_____

_____

_____

_____

_____

What have you learned during this time with Lord?

_____

_____

_____

_____

_____

Are there things you need to do differently?

_____

_____

_____

_____

_____

Before you leave this moment, write down God's directions to you.

_____

_____

_____

_____

_____

Close this journaling moment with a prayer.

_____

_____

_____

_____

_____

_____

I Am There In So Many Ways

—————— ❧ ——————

God created hearts so that blood could flow through and declare our existence

That little organ within our body is what allows us to survive our life span distance

Every vein and nerve within were intricately created to orchestrate a flow for our body

It's construction, only God could create. It endures unlike some equipment that is shoddy

The God created a miracle. Within a mom he created another life for some and twin lives for others

He decided what each family needed, whether it would be twin sisters or twin brothers

To each he gave that little life pumping organ that regulates our source of being

But there is one amazing thing that little organ does, you can feel, but its powers are not for seeing

You can be miles apart, yet in your heart you feel love of others, you think about them and you heart beats

Blood rushes to your head your brain takes you back to your beginning and the last time you shared side by side seats

You remember how many times that heart allowed you to feel each other's pain, victories, and the day college start

You remember the bond between you that is unbreakable and realized that you shared blood from your mom's heart

At this time in your life, you go through a separation, it's just a process, it will not be the thing that will tear you apart.

It will make you stronger!

🖉 God's word is powerful. What does this scripture say to you?

_____

_____

_____

_____

_____

🖉 What have you learned during this time with Lord?

_____

_____

_____

_____

_____

🖉 Are there things you need to do differently?

_____

_____

_____

_____

_____

🖉 Before you leave this moment, write down God's directions to you.

_____

_____

_____

_____

_____

🖉 Close this journaling moment with a prayer.

_____

_____

_____

_____

_____

Above All I Have,
I See You, Lord

*Now faith is confidence in what we hope for
and assurance about what we do not see.*

(HEBREWS 11:1 NASB)

So many wrong things have happened, Lord, I wonder how the day
will go
I am assured of this, that no matter what, you are in charge and all
things you know
I have to replace my doubts with thanksgiving and praise
What I have gone through is just a step on my way to strength, really, it's
just a phase

I already know that things will come to challenge my faith and trust in
you
It is my ultimate desire to please you, looking at the challenges will not
get me through
When I am diligently seeking your attitude and responses, you will
reward my diligence
Attentiveness to you word in my heart, will yield my reward and my
unshakable defense

Above all that I think, feel or anticipate, I have to alternate replacement
faith in my Lord
No matter how big the encounters, tasks, you expand my territory, you
are my life chord
You have ignited my history with evidence of your grace, mercy and
strength

No matter what happened in my life, you are always there, for me, you will go the length

Therefore, I tell you, whatever you ask for in prayer, believe that you have received it, and it will be yours (Mark 11:24)

Written as God so skillfully planted his words inside my heart and my thought and my being. I needed that Lord on 10/21/19 @ Dr. Cynthia Locke Henderson

(/) God's word is powerful. What does this scripture say to you?

_____

_____

_____

_____

_____

(/) What have you learned during this time with Lord?

_____

_____

_____

_____

_____

(/) Are there things you need to do differently?

_____

_____

_____

_____

_____

(/) Before you leave this moment, write down God's directions to you.

_____

_____

_____

_____

_____

(/) Close this journaling moment with a prayer.

_____

_____

_____

_____

_____

_____

My Anticipation Is YOU

Know that the LORD Himself is God; It is He who has made us, and
not we ourselves; We are His people and the sheep of His pasture.

(Psalms 100:3 NASB)

Lord, what do you do when you don't know what to do
I find myself trying to make things happen, that frequently does not
work, for you always get me through
Why do we have to go through so many cycles before we realize what to
do is not up to me
I needlessly wander around trying to work it out when it is not my battle
to fight, lose, or win, I have to let it be

Lord, what do I do when I don't know what to say
The battle in my mind goes back and forth thinking of responses that is
not your way
Sometimes words come out that should not have been said because
those words can't come back
Lord, you write the script for my life, I simply need to follow your direction which tells me how to act

Deep in my heart, can't help but think "WWJD", because your plans have
guided my walk again and again
Whey I open my mouth to give you thanks, bless your holy name and
call on you in the midst of pain
You bring your word back to my memory, so that I can get out of the
way and allow you to do what you do
Lord, my tank runs on empty in these situations as I wait in anticipation
of you

You never fail me, please forgive me for failing you!

But when the Father sends the Advocate as my representative—that is, the Holy Spirit—he will teach you everything and will remind you of everything I have told you (John 14:26 NLT)

Written a day after I had the joy of seeing God move mountain, trample the enemy under foot, and grace all things to work together on 10/21/2019 @ Dr. Cynthia Locke Henderson

God's word is powerful. What does this scripture say to you?

_____

_____

_____

_____

_____

What have you learned during this time with Lord?

_____

_____

_____

_____

_____

Are there things you need to do differently?

_____

_____

_____

_____

_____

Before you leave this moment, write down God's directions to you.

_____

_____

_____

_____

_____

Close this journaling moment with a prayer.

_____

_____

_____

_____

_____

There Is Nothing To Be Said Except Thank You

Lord, you are the unfailing All for every walk in this journey that I am on
You have allowed me to walk within myself and see what happens when it feels like I am in the day's dawn
You have allowed me to consider my responses when things and people around me come to destroy
You continue to reveal you are for me despite what I may feel or see, for you are always who you are

You are a force that man cannot control, regulate, switch on and off and definitely can't overpower
You remain consistent no matter what seems impossible, you are there my every hour
You put me in places that initially seem fearful, difficult, overpowering and consuming
Every action in those places have a purpose of destruction, hurting and dooming

Then you show yourself as my father, my daddy, my Lord, my Savior, my king, my AM that I Am
You give me the desires of my heart when I pray, you release the waters of grace's dam
You become for me a river of life, unstoppable, unmovable, ever flowing and refreshing with kindness
You Lord, always give me confidence that I am never alone, you write the test and help be your best

THANK YOU, LORD!!!!!!!

Written when I came before God exhausted with only the power to say "Thank You" on
10/24/19 @ Dr. Cynthia Locke Henderson

_/_ God's word is powerful. What does this scripture say to you?

_____
_____
_____
_____
_____

_/_ What have you learned during this time with Lord?

_____
_____
_____
_____
_____

_/_ Are there things you need to do differently?

_____
_____
_____
_____
_____

_/_ Before you leave this moment, write down God's directions to you.

_____
_____
_____
_____
_____

_/_ Close this journaling moment with a prayer.

_____
_____
_____
_____
_____

You Raised Me Up Beyond Mountains

———— ❧ ————

For I hold you by your right hand— I, the LORD your God. And I say to you, 'Don't be afraid. I am here to help you.

(ISAIAH 41:13 NLT)

Lord, mountains were strategically placed in my path to block what you had destined for me to execute
The mountains were placed in such a way that I had to either give in or wage a dispute
I found myself in a place where my health, my materials, my technology was engaged in the warfare
Lord, it seemed like massive confusion and attacks from everywhere

I was in a place where impossible seemed to be king and defeat was the queen destined to deliver me to a pit
Attacks came from the left and right, however, I heard your voice telling me, "This is the way walk in it"
I'm so glad to have you as my Savior and King because the situations only made me praise you more
You unlocked the door where there was a sign that said "You can't get through", you broke the door

I called out to you as my health seemed to feel the punch and my spirit could do nothing but praise thee
Lord you taught me how to refuse to give up, refuse to be destroyed, refuse to let mountains stop me
Lord it seemed you dispersed angels from all directions to create a restoring fountain

In the end you raised me up against the short, the tall, and even the thick mountains

You Lord raised me up so I can stand on mountains

Written during my time with God as I acknowledged the power and purpose, he has in me. I am truly love by God on 10/28/19 Dr. Cynthia Locke Henderson

God's word is powerful. What does this scripture say to you?

_____

_____

_____

_____

_____

What have you learned during this time with Lord?

_____

_____

_____

_____

_____

Are there things you need to do differently?

_____

_____

_____

_____

_____

Before you leave this moment, write down God's directions to you.

_____

_____

_____

_____

_____

Close this journaling moment with a prayer.

_____

_____

_____

_____

_____

My Help Comes From You Lord

My help comes from the LORD, the Maker of heaven and earth.

(PSALMS 121:2)

These eyes that you created for me to see both good in people I know and people I don't know, they also see the bad,
This heart that you created makes me feel the happy things in life and others and the feelings of others that's sad
I have lived in and out of experiences that make me question so many things that I witness and know that it is wrong
I have lived through events that help me witness your greatness and compassion, those encounters make me strong

This thing called racism is an ugly and malicious beast that causes a tremendous amount of inquiry within my being
I have seen it hurt, change lives, harm vast sums of people, change their thinking and cause extensive disagreeing
Lord, I know you strategically place us in places where we can make a better impact if we are not weary and faint
Responding to its ugly existence sometimes makes it difficult to hold our peace and remain in a state of restraint

You have purpose for me, you endured things worse than what I see, feel, or encounter, wondering if it can be healed
Lord, I look to you to help me play my role in what I do and what I say within your grace that keeps me sealed
Lord, I look to you to help show that your love on the cross was extended for all races

Lord help me reach the hearts and not forsake my purpose because of the diversity in hearts and on faces

May I never forget who my help comes from as I look to you

So do not fear, for I am with you; do not be dismayed, for I am your God. I will strengthen you and help you; I will uphold you with my righteous right hand (Isaiah 41:10)

God's word is powerful. What does this scripture say to you?

_____

_____

_____

_____

_____

What have you learned during this time with Lord?

_____

_____

_____

_____

_____

Are there things you need to do differently?

_____

_____

_____

_____

_____

Before you leave this moment, write down God's directions to you.

_____

_____

_____

_____

Close this journaling moment with a prayer.

_____

_____

_____

_____

_____

I Am Enough

And God is able to make all grace abound toward you; that ye, always having all sufficiency in all things, may abound to every good work.

(2 CORINTHIANS 9:8 KJV)

Lord, thank you for daily letting me know, that you created me to be enough
And when I don't measure up to be who man wants, you encourage me to be tough
There are times when all you want from me is to be still, knowing that you have all I need
There has not been a situation when I was alone; so, when others desire that I fall, I must not concede

Lord, it gets rough and repetitive dealing with the chipping away of me; this person you created
It gets dishearten when nothing is ever enough and with all the acts of malice and hatred
Yet I have to look through blinded thoughts of proving myself to man, before I see, you designed me for today
And no matter what is thrown my way, I may look like a tree that has been bent, bark chipped away

Like the tree, leaves fall, but new ones come to fill the spaces, branches fall but it is you who replace them all
I am still in flesh and yes, some things may have me bent over as if I am going to fall
But you make sure that despite the enemy's plan, I will stand and stand still
For after each season in my life, you give me confidence that I am enough as long as I am in your will

I am not cheap; I was bought with a price that man can never pay.
You paid for me on the cross! You made me enough

_/_ God's word is powerful. What does this scripture say to you?

_____

_____

_____

_____

_____

_/_ What have you learned during this time with Lord?

_____

_____

_____

_____

_____

_/_ Are there things you need to do differently?

_____

_____

_____

_____

_____

_/_ Before you leave this moment, write down God's directions to you.

_____

_____

_____

_____

_____

_/_ Close this journaling moment with a prayer.

_____

_____

_____

_____

_____

_____

Where Would I Be If It Were Not For You Lord

———— ❧ ————

I have been crucified with Christ and I no longer live, but Christ lives in me. The life I now live in the body, I live by faith in the Son of God, who loved me and gave himself for me.

(GALATIANS 2:20)

Lord, life has been hard, but you did not let it take me away before my time or destroy me
You knew the sickness, the accidents, the hatred and the strife against me before I came to be
You knew whether I would struggle and give up without trying or resisting
You knew how much I could take even when warfare against me was persisting

I was child number two which gave my mom a chance to learn about mothering before I came
Grandma died just as I was born, who would teach her to be my mom, there was no blame
Because you Lord preserved the wisdom passed down from her mom and love equally passed on
Many of things of value were taken or sold, she had no one to call on for her mom was gone

Lord, with such a limitation of people, money, things, and just one faithful friend, you allowed her to mother
She came to love you, trust you for healing her illness, trust you for making a way and counting on no other

You gave her what she needed to teach her children wisdom, how to grow their gifts and how to care

I am her because of the miracle of life that lived long enough teach me and show me that you are everywhere

I have had to go through trying and treacherous valleys and in the shadows of death

I have been without, only to learn that you will not let me suffer lack for you are my source of wealth

You placed in me grandma and momma's wisdom overlaid with your grace and mercy based in salvation

I now realize that I am who I am, where I am supposed to be, doing what you want, for I am your creation

Written as inspired by God, when I thought about the "What Ifs" in my life. I realized that God had a bigger plan for me 10/20/2019 © Dr. Cynthia Locke Henderson

✏ God's word is powerful. What does this scripture say to you?

_____
_____
_____
_____
_____

✏ What have you learned during this time with Lord?

_____
_____
_____
_____
_____

✏ Are there things you need to do differently?

_____
_____
_____
_____
_____

✏ Before you leave this moment, write down God's directions to you.

_____
_____
_____
_____
_____

✏ Close this journaling moment with a prayer.

_____
_____
_____
_____
_____

The Lord Is My Conductor

I am the vine; you are the branches. If you remain in me and I in you,
you will bear much fruit; apart from me you can do nothing

(JOHN 15:5)

There are times my days seem like a ride on a train to a specific
destination
It seems like a long ride; however, you will arrive where you are going if
you withstand the duration
Sometimes you are tired of the rolling and rocking and seeing desolate
places
You look around and see all sort of expressions on others faces

I have often looked at older people and ask that you get them safely to
where they are going
I pray for peace when they arrive, strength when they walk out because
each step seems slowing
I pray for the young ones that they are not consumed by a world that
offers more than they need
I pray for you to give them wisdom to know the difference from needs
and poisonous seeds

Lord, I offer prayer for direction as I ride this train with the faith that you
will get me to that place in life
When I am able to overcome going through places that look like life has
dried up leaving struggles and strife
 I pray that I am not tempted to get off at the wrong station because of
impatience and when things are severe
Lord I ride this train to my destined destination you have for me; I pray
that I hear your directions are clear

I don't always know where my trip will take me, but I trust that you are my conductor and will get me to where I am supposed to be

Written as I yielded my life to my conductor on my train ride through life. 11/1/2019
© Dr. Cynthia Locke Henderson

✏️ God's word is powerful. What does this scripture say to you?

_____
_____
_____
_____
_____

✏️ What have you learned during this time with Lord?

_____
_____
_____
_____
_____

✏️ Are there things you need to do differently?

_____
_____
_____
_____
_____

✏️ Before you leave this moment, write down God's directions to you.

_____
_____
_____
_____
_____

✏️ Close this journaling moment with a prayer.

_____
_____
_____
_____
_____

You Are There Every Time

The mind governed by the flesh is death, but the mind governed by the Spirit is life and peace.

(ROMANS 8:6)

Though my mind made me feel fatherless, Lord, you are the father that never left my side
You have been there through my learning pain, my celebratory times, and during all those times I cried
No matter the complications of where I have been emotionally or physically, you were present
When I did not have the things, I thought I needed, you covered me and made known your intent

There have been times that I thought I could not fit you into my agenda or have a place on my list
Lord, there were times my anger took over and refused to acknowledge you were in the midst
You have been like my lighthouse, shining you list and signaling danger ahead
Dissecting tricks of the enemy woven in covers, you expose the enemy down to the last thread

Lord, I first ask your forgiveness for every time I tried to fix things alone as if you were not there
Please forgive me for allowing moments of aloneness to consume me making me feel you did not care
Thank you for maintaining the source of my strength, my peace, my direction, the consistency in despair
Thank you for mending the broken places in my dreams, my peace, my trust, I know you were always there

Written as I gave careful consideration to God who has been consistent in my life from my beginning to know. Lord I thank you on n11/4/19 © Dr. Cynthia Locke Henderson

God's word is powerful. What does this scripture say to you?

_____

_____

_____

_____

_____

What have you learned during this time with Lord?

_____

_____

_____

_____

_____

Are there things you need to do differently?

_____

_____

_____

_____

_____

Before you leave this moment, write down God's directions to you.

_____

_____

_____

_____

_____

Close this journaling moment with a prayer.

_____

_____

_____

_____

_____

_____

Lord, You Opened Doors, Help Me Accomplish Your Will

I know your deeds. See, I have placed before you an open door
that no one can shut. I know that you have little strength, yet you
have kept my word and have not denied my name.

(REVELATIONS 3:8)

Lord, you woke me up this morning for an open door that you placed
before me

No one knows the reasons; it is an opportunity that is between me and
thee

You have placed me in valley experiences, only to take me to the top of
mountains

I have been through experiences that flow with hatred but this time you
are taking me before free running fountains

Lord, I trust you to bring things back to my memory what you want said
and really heard

Lord, measure out my emotions in a purposeful way, give me a penetrating and powerful word

Today you put me in a place where I am but one, speaking on the behalf
of so many

Lord, please help say what helps the children, their parents, the people
that work with them, let me not leave out any

Lord, your word is hidden in my heart for today a door has been opened
that no one can shut

Lord I am the ambassador for today, help me make connections that no one, no politician can cut

Lord I look to you for my strength, your wisdom, your powerful simplicity and clarity, for your will is the main

Some look to their personal strength, to hold the door open, but Jesus I believe in the power of your Name

God's word is powerful. What does this scripture say to you?

_____
_____
_____
_____
_____

What have you learned during this time with Lord?

_____
_____
_____
_____
_____

Are there things you need to do differently?

_____
_____
_____
_____
_____

Before you leave this moment, write down God's directions to you.

_____
_____
_____
_____
_____

Close this journaling moment with a prayer.

_____
_____
_____
_____
_____

Lord, I Belong To You

I praise you because I am fearfully and wonderfully made; your works are wonderful; I know that full well.

(PSALM 139:14)

Lord, you made the heavens and every celestial item that moves within it and intertwine
To the stars you gave commands of when to shine, to the moon when to move forward and shine,
To the sun you told it when to give heat and when to give light, and when to brighten dark places in the morning
To the sun, when to hide its face and allow clouds to lessen the light and let water dry places when it is storming

In the midst of your creation, you created animals that filled the rivers, skies and the earth - inside and out
Then you created man, woman and gave them freedom to move, run, and walk about
Lord, in your creation you had me on the blue print and allowed me entrance at your appointed moment
I came to a 16-year-old girl who was losing her mother to death and a household with must to lament

Lord, it was in the midst of this that you implemented your plan, and allowed me to come forth in this domain
Only you knew the paths that I would take, the storms I'd survive, or what it took to reach intended gains
You were identified as my Savior and father very early in my life, a connection that I never lost and needed to survive
You touch others to be a resource to me as I grow, but through it all, I belong to you, you are the reason that I will thrive

When it is all said and done, resources come and go I belong to you, you are my source

So do not fear, for I am with you; do not be dismayed, for I am your God. I will strengthen you and help you; I will uphold you with my righteous right hand. (Isaiah 41:10)

Written during my time with God when helped me understand, thou the battle is active, I am his child, I am part of his plan, I have connection. This is my birth month

© *11/6/2019. Dr. Cynthia Locke Henderson*

God's word is powerful. What does this scripture say to you?

_____

_____

_____

_____

_____

What have you learned during this time with Lord?

_____

_____

_____

_____

_____

Are there things you need to do differently?

_____

_____

_____

_____

_____

Before you leave this moment, write down God's directions to you.

_____

_____

_____

_____

_____

Close this journaling moment with a prayer.

_____

_____

_____

_____

_____

Wonderful Things Happen When You "Be Still"

My soul, wait silently for God alone, for my expectation is from Him

(Psalm 62:5 NKJV)

God is ever present when you steal moments of retreat from trying to fix things yourself
If you have noticed he gives and supplies without us trying to do things out of his will to gain wealth
When loneliness fills your surrounds like a river that is overflowing and has no end
Be still, be silent, in this place with just you and the Lord, he tells you how to overcome and win

In this place turn off worrying, hurting, despair, and feelings of wanting this loneliness to cease
Reflect on his word that says, "I am with you always", for he will mend your brokenness and replace it with peace
I know there are times you move from one crisis to the next without taking a break
You feel compelled to do something, say something, listen to his voice as he be bids you be still and wait

In this place of stillness, realize that he has covered you in and out of turmoil, he has brought you this far
He knows the growing pains that you have gone through, the growth you have made to have you where you are
Remember the person you used to be, the troubling responses you gave when things seemed to go wrong

This too shall pass, be still and listen for God to speak peace to your heart and give you strength that will make you strong

Lord may I never forget to wait and be still!

Written in my still place with the Lord, in my moments of expectations on 11/ 7/2019 ©
Dr. Cynthia Locke Henderson

🖊 God's word is powerful. What does this scripture say to you?

_____
_____
_____
_____
_____

🖊 What have you learned during this time with Lord?

_____
_____
_____
_____
_____

🖊 Are there things you need to do differently?

_____
_____
_____
_____
_____

🖊 Before you leave this moment, write down God's directions to you.

_____
_____
_____
_____
_____

🖊 Close this journaling moment with a prayer.

_____
_____
_____
_____
_____

Complexity
Fight With Praise

———— ❧ ————

But the Advocate, the Holy Spirit, whom the Father will send in my
name, will teach you all things and will remind you of everything
I have said to you.

(JOHN 14:26)

Some days begin with questions, uneasiness, no directions, reflections on the "WHYs" in my world
I often wonder why is it necessary for people to be so mean spirited and
frequently throwing devious swirls
Why are they so intimidated by others instead of focused on their world,
there is enough room for them to be who they are
It gets complex trying to figure out why they do what they do and why
do they take this hatred so far

Lord, it is after I go through this cycle of thinking about the complexity
of hate that I have used the power of your name
Wasting too much time wondering is loss time that I have to fight with
praise because you are my aim
Some of the encounters seem to pierce my soul, seize my tears, and
attempt to take my peace
I am so grateful for the power of your words and the power in your
name that at times makes it cease

Lord, I hunger for consistency with responding the way you want me to
Lord, I hunger for allowing you to order my steps, order my thoughts
with everything I do
You promised in your work that you would fill me when I thirst for your
righteousness

Lord, it is complex, but not enough for me to give up, Lord continue to be with me as I do my best

For all who are led by the Spirit of God are sons of God. For you did not receive a spirit of slavery that returns you to fear, but you received the Spirit of sonship, by whom we cry, "Abba! Father!"
(Romans 8:14-15 BSB)

Written during my time with the Lord. He untangled my complex feelings and thoughts,
11/8/2019 © Dr. Cynthia L. Henderson

God's word is powerful. What does this scripture say to you?

_____

_____

_____

_____

_____

What have you learned during this time with Lord?

_____

_____

_____

_____

_____

Are there things you need to do differently?

_____

_____

_____

_____

_____

Before you leave this moment, write down God's directions to you.

_____

_____

_____

_____

_____

Close this journaling moment with a prayer.

_____

_____

_____

_____

_____

Lord I Believe

"Truly I tell you, if anyone says to this mountain,
'Go, throw yourself into the sea,' and does not doubt in their heart but
believes that what they say will happen, it will be done for them."

(MARK 11:23)

Lord, I've searched inside of me, to see if I really believe and trust you
When I look back at all that I have been through
no man, no power on this earth
Could have made a decision regarding what would come my way after
my birth

I have been on this earth for quite some time
So many battles have been waged in my mind
Yet, frequently I have to look back before I can trust your control over
me
Frequently, I try, I fail, I give up, I walk away, before I realize the solution
is in thee

Lord, I know so much about you, but the complete story has not been told
The aches, the pain, the forgetting, the remembering after a time lets me
know I am getting old
I know these things by signs and events that in my life you weave
Lord, I want to trust you without reservation and inquiry Lord I want
you to know, *In You I Believe*

Lord in this birthday month I don't know what you have in store for me
I thank you for getting me here and Lord I yield my life to you, I come
willingly and free
My assurance as I enter another year is that I cannot go it without you
front and center

For every valley that comes, every door you open, every trial that comes, I know you are there saying, it's ok *ENTER*

Lord you are my strength!

Therefore, I tell you, whatever you ask for in prayer, believe that you have received it, and it will be yours. (Mark 11:24)

Written as God answered all the thoughts that travel in and out of my mine, in and out of time. 11/11/19 © Dr. Cynthia Locke Henderson

🖊 God's word is powerful. What does this scripture say to you?

_____

_____

_____

_____

_____

🖊 What have you learned during this time with Lord?

_____

_____

_____

_____

_____

🖊 Are there things you need to do differently?

_____

_____

_____

_____

_____

🖊 Before you leave this moment, write down God's directions to you.

_____

_____

_____

_____

_____

🖊 Close this journaling moment with a prayer.

_____

_____

_____

_____

_____

Today Is A New Day

I will make rivers flow on barren heights, and springs within the valleys. I will turn the desert into pools of water, and the parched ground into springs.

(ISAIAH 41:18)

Today is a day uniquely different from the other days that I exist
Today is a day that I live for you, anything different that is not what you want, please help me resist
Lord I awake with expectations of seeing some of your many **attributes**
Lord I yield myself, my day to you, you are **omniscient** you know how this day will compute

God, I know you are **omnipotent** and there are no limitations to what you offer me today
Let me be free of myself, my way of responding, my way of handling complexities, let me do today your way
Please allow me to embrace your **love** that has sustained me all of these years and deleted impacts of sin
No matter how discriminating acts may be, let me see things through your **righteous** eyes so that can win

I come to this day as your guest and give way to your **omnipresence** because you see what I can't see
God you are **immutable**, you have not changed, you said I am yours and highly favored that is what I want to be
You are my almighty God who has been **merciful** and destroy things that come to kill, still, destroy, and give strife
You have come that I might have life, you have come like a river of peace, cleansing, and flowing through my life

Lord thank you for the benefits your attributes, brought to me yesterday, today and forevermore.

God's word is powerful. What does this scripture say to you?

_____
_____
_____
_____
_____

What have you learned during this time with Lord?

_____
_____
_____
_____
_____

Are there things you need to do differently?

_____
_____
_____
_____
_____

Before you leave this moment, write down God's directions to you.

_____
_____
_____
_____
_____

Close this journaling moment with a prayer.

_____
_____
_____
_____
_____

Pray

Never stop praying.

(1 Thessalonians 5:17 NLT)

There is no replacement for the time you set aside and just pray
An opportunity to call in reinforcement when no solution seems to remedy your day
Prayer takes the venom from your anger and need to just say something
What you are about to say or do with angry intent will make the anger cling

The Lord sees and hears the turbulence in your situation whether you are right or have been made wrong
Holding on to disturbance in your life only comes to take you down as others see you are not strong
Each drop of vengeance does not belong to you it is only a test of your faith to what God has promised
Only prayer will bring that stronghold down, only prayer will bring you back to a state where you are the calmest

Prayer helps you stay in place so that God can show you his might and glory
Prayer is the key element that shows God is in control and he will help you change your story
Prayer wipes out anger, retribution, your need to make others see what you do
Remember your miracles are testimonies of what God can do, don't attempt to take his praise, it is not about you

Lord never let me forget about praying and asking you!

Call to me and I will answer you and tell you great and unsearchable things you do not know. (Jeremiah 33:3 NIV)

Written as God gave me for my sister and for me on 11/14/19 © Dr. Cynthia Locke Henderson

God's word is powerful. What does this scripture say to you?

_____

_____

_____

_____

_____

What have you learned during this time with Lord?

_____

_____

_____

_____

_____

Are there things you need to do differently?

_____

_____

_____

_____

_____

Before you leave this moment, write down God's directions to you.

_____

_____

_____

_____

_____

Close this journaling moment with a prayer.

_____

_____

_____

_____

_____

_____

You Are Immeasurable

Lord, I think of some of the things and times you have invested in
your servant
You have allowed me to rise above those that doubt that I am yours so
still I pray a prayer most fervent
Many can measure how many times I may fail at man's task
But they cannot measure how many times you have come to my rescue
when I ask

They measure how many times I have cried my way through dejections
and fears
Only God was there to eradicate the causes of my fears and wipe away
all my tears
You may think you have measured the times that you have seen me fall
Oh, but God turned those falls into an opportunity for others to see that
he can deliver me through them all

Numbers and the span of time does not matter to God because his
measurements go to infinity
His love and carefulness in growing me it goes to eternity
Therefore, who shall I fear when my savior is always near to give me my
special time
He has been my strength more times than I can imagine, he is there for
all his people and still uniquely mine

God I was born to love you, that I now clearly understand
You hold me up with your righteous right and protective hand
Man wonders what kind of God you are, how omnipresent you are, how
omnipotent you are

They can't hold a measuring stick next to you, they can't walk the miles to see you have brought me this far

You are immeasurable, boundlessness, you possess eternity and perpetuity, you are God

Written as truly inspired to praise and worship my Savior
11/15/2019 © Dr. Cynthia Locke Henderson

God's word is powerful. What does this scripture say to you?

_____

_____

_____

_____

_____

What have you learned during this time with Lord?

_____

_____

_____

_____

_____

Are there things you need to do differently?

_____

_____

_____

_____

_____

Before you leave this moment, write down God's directions to you.

_____

_____

_____

_____

_____

Close this journaling moment with a prayer.

_____

_____

_____

_____

_____

I Could Not Make It Without You

But as for me, I am poor and needy; come quickly to me, O God. You are my help and my deliverer; LORD, do not delay.

(PSALMS 70:5)

Lord, no matter how much I think I am in control of my daily program
I know that I need to acknowledge the spiritual presence of the Lamb
The Lamb knows what lies ahead in my day
When I pray, He speaks to me and directs me to respond a certain way

This is the day that the Lord has made and I will rejoice in it
And anything that comes my way I know that you will give me what I need to fit
I look at this day and see it as a day to rejoice in always and see opportunity to give praise
I cannot allow confusion and anger today; I have to replace it with a hallelujah phase

I commit to being free of me and focusing on glory
I commit to telling others of how you are changing my story
I am yours Lord and will not give what you blessed me with to another
I will focus more on uplifting and praying for my sisters and brothers

Written because I need God today, I cannot begin my day without Him
11/18/19 @ Dr. Cynthia Locke Henderson

God's word is powerful. What does this scripture say to you?

_____

_____

_____

_____

_____

What have you learned during this time with Lord?

_____

_____

_____

_____

_____

Are there things you need to do differently?

_____

_____

_____

_____

_____

Before you leave this moment, write down God's directions to you.

_____

_____

_____

_____

_____

Close this journaling moment with a prayer.

_____

_____

_____

_____

_____

Miracles Happen Non-Stop

Therefore, I tell you, whatever you ask for in prayer, believe that you have received it, and it will be yours.

(MARK 11:24)

Miracles happen when God intervenes for something that seems impossible
Miracles occur when diverse forces in our life seem unstoppable
Miracles occur every morning I awake from a sleep where my trust in God occurs
Our bodies stop for rest and all that happen on that day becomes an instant blur

Miracles happen when my anger is managed by God, I don't have to take revenge
Things that I want to do, things I could have done, responses I could have made dangle on an invisible hinge
I am allowed to feel human emotions, yet I must turn to God and remember his promise to fight my battles
The miracles happen when I am able to let go and let God because nothing else matters

Miracles happen when I wake and oxygen is moving through my lungs as God invites me into the day
Miracles happen when an accident is diverted away from me in a miraculous way
Shootings are happening rampantly, killing our children, people randomly, spreading that monster called fear
My miracles happen each day God keeps a bullet from finding me, keep mean-spirited acts far and not near

After all that I have been through my miracle is to be able to be here, this moment, this year

My miracle happens when the wind blows invisible to my eyes yet audible to my ear

Miracles happen because I am willing to trust my God who I can't see, yet he lives within my soul

My miracle is trusting him from my youth all through the years as I began to turn old

Lord you are my miracle maker!

Heal me, LORD, and I will be healed; save me and I will be saved, for you are the one I praise. (Jeremiah 17:14)

Written because God miraculous started my day with what I needed for what lie ahead in this day © 11/19/19, Dr. Cynthia Locke Henderson

🖊 God's word is powerful. What does this scripture say to you?

_____
_____
_____
_____
_____

🖊 What have you learned during this time with Lord?

_____
_____
_____
_____
_____

🖊 Are there things you need to do differently?

_____
_____
_____
_____
_____

🖊 Before you leave this moment, write down God's directions to you.

_____
_____
_____
_____
_____

🖊 Close this journaling moment with a prayer.

_____
_____
_____
_____
_____

Nothing Can Keep My God Away from Me

—— ❧ ——

Surely, he will save you from the fowler's snare and
from the deadly pestilence.
He will cover you with his feathers, and under his wings you will find
refuge; his faithfulness will be your shield and rampart.

(PSALM 91:3-4)

When confusion is all around me trying to grab me into its controls
When evil tries to take my focus and cause anger to unfold
When traps are laid before me, beside me and behind me
When attacks come to take me down in ways that I can't see

God is omniscient and knows everything and his knowledge is complete
I am his heir and child he has answers and solutions that nothing and no
one can beat
I don't need to hide, be consumed by fear, nor am I out of His view and
the heart of my Lord
I am covered because he is omnipresent his coverage of me and what I
go through is very broad

Fear can't overtake me because God is my refuge, my strength and my
strong tower
I am covered with the wings of the Lord even when hatred, evil, and
deception fall like a rain shower
When I cry visibly or deep within in my heart, God turns my mourning
of pain into a song and dance of praise
Nothing and no one can take me on a mountain to see how far I can fall
or in a valley where I can't be raised

I was bought with a price that man can never pay, because man can't keep my God away from me

For He will give His angels charge concerning you, To guard you in all your ways. They will bear you up in their hands, That you do not strike your foot against a stone. (Psalm 91:11-12 NASB 1995)

Written as completely inspired by God who has decreed victory on this day. © 11/20/19
Dr. Cynthia Locke Henderson

God's word is powerful. What does this scripture say to you?

_____
_____
_____
_____
_____

What have you learned during this time with Lord?

_____
_____
_____
_____
_____

Are there things you need to do differently?

_____
_____
_____
_____
_____

Before you leave this moment, write down God's directions to you.

_____
_____
_____
_____
_____

Close this journaling moment with a prayer.

_____
_____
_____
_____
_____

Have I Told You Lately, How Much I Love You

Lord, I stop at this time in my life to adore you and thank you for being my Master

You have been in and out of my struggles and my personal life disasters

You have fearfully and wonderfully made me in such a way that I am still here

I have gone through different levels of aloneness and finally commit to knowing you will always be near

I have missed a lot of things in life, some I felt that I must have and felt they were absolutely necessary

You, Lord, granted my needs and wants and some things were sent my way for me to pray and tarry

You made life as easy as it needed to be for me to learn and for your power to show

You also made some parts of my life hard and seemingly unbearable to allow me to grow

This is a time that I honor and worship you for being the only father that I have ever had

I missed having my father and knowing him as the man to call dad

Today I realized all the things I sometimes take for granted and give little thought

Today I realized that you are filling all of my gaps and making my life be what it ought

So, Lord have I told you lately that I love You?

Those who live according to the flesh have their minds set on what the flesh desires; but those who live in accordance with the Spirit have their minds set on what the Spirit desires. (Romans 8:5)

God's word is powerful. What does this scripture say to you?

_____
_____
_____
_____
_____

What have you learned during this time with Lord?

_____
_____
_____
_____
_____

Are there things you need to do differently?

_____
_____
_____
_____
_____

Before you leave this moment, write down God's directions to you.

_____
_____
_____
_____
_____

Close this journaling moment with a prayer.

_____
_____
_____
_____
_____

You Are My Source

I Know That I Am Nothing Without You
I Know That I Am Nothing Without You
I Know That I Am Nothing Without You
I Know That I Am Nothing Without You
I Know That I Am Nothing Without You
I Know That I Am Nothing Without You
I Know That I Am Nothing Without You
I Know That I Am Nothing Without You
I Know That I Am Nothing Without You
I Know That I Am Nothing Without You
I Know That I Am Nothing Without You
I Know That I Am Nothing Without You
I Know That I Am Nothing Without You
I Know That I Am Nothing Without You
I Know That I Am Nothing Without You
I Know That I Am Nothing Without You
I Know That I Am Nothing Without You
I Know That I Am Nothing Without You
I Know That I Am Nothing Without You
I Know That I Am Nothing Without You
I Know That I Am Nothing Without You
I Know That I Am Nothing Without You
I Need You Lord
I Need You Lord
I Need You Lord
I Need You Lord
I Need You Lord
I Need You Lord
I Need You Lord
I Need You Lord
I Need You Lord

God's word is powerful. What does this scripture say to you?

_____

_____

_____

_____

_____

What have you learned during this time with Lord?

_____

_____

_____

_____

_____

Are there things you need to do differently?

_____

_____

_____

_____

_____

Before you leave this moment, write down God's directions to you.

_____

_____

_____

_____

_____

Close this journaling moment with a prayer.

_____

_____

_____

_____

_____

Why Should I Feel Discouraged?

———— ⚜ ————

Stand firm then, with the belt of truth buckled around your waist, with the breastplate of righteousness in place, and with your feet fitted with the readiness that comes from the gospel of peace.

(EPHESIANS 6:14-15)

Why should I feel discouraged given the Lord's commitment to keep my salvation? Though circumstances come in diverse ways trying to alter my determination and God's manifestation

Why should the shadows of dread and darkness come to block my focus on God's son?

When God has fought battle after battle, wiped tear after tear, and allowed me to see all he has won

Why should my heart feel lonely without anyone to stand by my side and be there for me to touch?

When he speaks his promises through the word, through songs, through friends - he has done so much

God replenishes the earth planting seeds that I don't see, with new births, with all sorts of animals, even the sparrow

He orders the seconds, minutes, hours, days, months, years, no matter if my path is wide or narrow

I have no right, no reason, no purpose to ever allow discouragement to take away what God has invested

Interruptions will come, people will come to try us, challenges never stop, I will be repeatedly tested

I must stand firm, put on the breast plate of righteousness, and buckle

up with truth and never allow, my prayers to cease
For as I surrender my all to you, withholding nothing I know that you
replace discouragement with peace

*Discouragement has no power unless I give it power. I choose this day to
put my trust in God who meets when I am in his presence.*

God's word is powerful. What does this scripture say to you?

_____

_____

_____

_____

_____

What have you learned during this time with Lord?

_____

_____

_____

_____

_____

Are there things you need to do differently?

_____

_____

_____

_____

_____

Before you leave this moment, write down God's directions to you.

_____

_____

_____

_____

_____

Close this journaling moment with a prayer.

_____

_____

_____

_____

_____

Life is Like A Spiral

Call to me and I will answer you and tell you great and unsearchable things you do not know.

(JEREMIAH 33:3)

Life feels like a spiral spinning endlessly around and around from one point to the next without disconnect
We know that our beginning is with you Lord, we have chosen, as we begin to focus on you, and the world we reject
As we go down the spiraling path, some areas gradually widening and tightening testing our commitment
We sometimes get stuck in the spiral wondering if our behavior is what you desire and what you want us to represent

As I look back at how far you have brought me, I can always remember spirally back to your mercy and grace
I remember how great your faithfulness is towards me, you are my refuge when life's spiral tightens, you are in my space
There are no areas in my life spiral that are not covered by your forgiveness, your love, and patience
You loosen Satan's attempt to squeeze the life from me, you rescue me you are my defense

I have no need to hurt to keep from being hurt, no need for self-destruction, no need to fight, the battle is not mine
Your will is that I prosper and be healthy as my soul prospers, despite what part of the spiral I am in, you make me shine
It is when I pray and humble myself that you hear me and heal the injury, I receive you in my life spiral
You are my king, my rock, my strength, my redeemer, my shield, my sustainer, you are my survival

Life will happen, it is supposed to happen, that is part of the course, no matter how or where it spirals
You are There!

If my people, who are called by my name, will humble themselves and pray and seek my face and turn from their wicked ways, then I will hear from heaven, and I will forgive their sin and will heal their land (2 Chronicles 7:14)

In the presence of the Lord, I asked for his help because the spiral of life tightens and I need his help. He responded 11/26/2019 © Dr. Cynthia Locke Henderson

🖊 God's word is powerful. What does this scripture say to you?

_____
_____
_____
_____
_____

🖊 What have you learned during this time with Lord?

_____
_____
_____
_____
_____

🖊 Are there things you need to do differently?

_____
_____
_____
_____
_____

🖊 Before you leave this moment, write down God's directions to you.

_____
_____
_____
_____
_____

🖊 Close this journaling moment with a prayer.

_____
_____
_____
_____
_____

You Are God Alone And There is None Comparable

In everything give thanks: for this is the will of God in
Christ Jesus concerning you.

(1 THESSALONIANS 5:18 KJV)

I am because you are, I am who I am because of you, you are the writer
of my story
No one can claim playwright of how the events unfolded in my life, you
deserve all the glory
You were in between the pages of every new day, making sure I followed
the script
There were times when trauma entered the pages, those scenes I wanted
to simply rip

You know my beginnings, my betweenness, and you know that the
performance of my life is not over yet
Many are the miracles and wonders in some of the scenes, frequent are
the productions to cause threats
Some left before the final story thinking that the story had ended, not
yet says the Lord there is more to come
When the audiences in my life thought that I was done, God said I will
keep my promise to her until the play is done

He elevated her from scenes of sickness, he let her dwell among those
that wanted to see her fail and fall
He placed her in scenes to care for others some who thought themselves
greater and some that were small
He allowed her to bless the forgotten in scenes of despair, scenes of

lonely places whether others needed her to care
God allowed her story to display God's compassion for his people no matter where

The grand finality is yet to come, for she will not stop performing until God says well done
Scenes are still being written, showing how merciful God is and the battles waiting to be won
The Lord is the playwriter of her story, he is her scene designer and he will continue to set the stage
God and God alone has allowed her to reach this appointed time and he alone will write the final page

You Lord, and you alone have never left me nor forsaken me,
I will not forget

From the character to the playwriter, I give you glory as you unfold my story. 11/27/19
© Dr. Cynthia Locke Henderson

God's word is powerful. What does this scripture say to you?

_____

_____

_____

_____

_____

What have you learned during this time with Lord?

_____

_____

_____

_____

_____

Are there things you need to do differently?

_____

_____

_____

_____

_____

Before you leave this moment, write down God's directions to you.

_____

_____

_____

_____

_____

Close this journaling moment with a prayer.

_____

_____

_____

_____

_____

_____

Thanks Giving

This is the day when I watch those who I have loved receive concern and care
It is not just the food set before them, its the moment the world stops to demonstrate God's love everywhere
It is the time when the homeless person is reminded that you are not alone growing old
It is the time when the fear of being harmed, forgotten, cut off from life, and fear of dying because of the cold

Lord, help us remember the stranger on the street living in a tent with all of their worth packed in a bag or box
Help us remember that, but for your grace any of us could be in the same place, treasuring the right and left sock
Help us remember them, help us remember that a simple smile to them permeates their core, down to their soul
Remember that thanksgiving is lifelong and recognizing that what is little to us may translate to a gift to fit in their roll

The extra blanket on my shelf can warm a lady or man that has fallen to hard times and suffering lack
That coat, hung in my closet unused, crowding space, could be just the one that's needed to warm a person's back
Lord, there's no price tag on a smile, nor for giving a friendly "hello", sharing my blessing to have and not need
You destined me to show love, to care, to give, to let someone know your love and you are using me to plant a seed

Lord. I pray that the seeds fall on fertile ground and it is the seed that brings them from that dark place.

Lord, I pray that they understand that your grace and mercy is available in their space

Lord, I yield my time to reach out expecting nothing in return

Lord, more than anything else I pray that your love for that homeless person, lets them know you are concerned

Lord thank you for making your plans for me clear. Thank you for the strength follow your plans. 11/29/19 © Dr. Cynthia Locke Henderson

God's word is powerful. What does this scripture say to you?

_____

_____

_____

_____

_____

What have you learned during this time with Lord?

_____

_____

_____

_____

_____

Are there things you need to do differently?

_____

_____

_____

_____

_____

Before you leave this moment, write down God's directions to you.

_____

_____

_____

_____

_____

Close this journaling moment with a prayer.

_____

_____

_____

_____

_____

I Can't Fill The Gaps In Life

Lord, I have spent a life time trying to fill the vacant places in my lifespan
I tried to make myself be the person that everyone likes dumping my identify and fitting into their plan
And still you watched over me
Lord, I looked for others to take the pain away and give me peace
Nothing I did gave peace as the pain within and without never seemed to completely cease
And still you watched over me
I took some of the blows of life thinking if I allowed myself to sacrifice for others
Yet the holes in my life where hidden so that no one would uncover
And still you watched over me
I attempted to replace the gaps, trying to learn enough to fill the spaces
Starving for the looks of others at what I accomplished, seeing the smiles on their faces
And still you watched over me
I found myself in places of aloneness and trying to make the best of it
Yet friends only came to use me, take all that you blessed me with taking every bit
And still you watched over me
In my plight of trying to fill the gap I heard that a baby was born to redeem the world
He had a purpose in my life, he would get the glory and my world he would unfurl
And still you watched over me

He exposed me to the power of the Bible, His word, His love for me and listening to my many pleas

He began filling the empty spaces and filling the gaps and talking to me as I talked to him on my bended knees

And still you watched over me

It was not long before I realized that baby boy did not come just to give me presents on his birthday

He came in my youth, as I grew, as I matriculated, as I stopped trying to be my god and doing things his way

And still you watched over me

Things continued to occur, but I reacted differently, I replaced my desire with the things that celebrated his birth

He gave me promises of peace, He came in my darkness and promised me light as I live on this earth

And still you watched over me

As I walk in increasing faith that I am never alone and that it is not my job to fix me

I now remember that he is preserving me for thee

And still you watched over me

Written as definitely comforted by God 12/2/2019 © Dr. Cynthia Locke Henderson

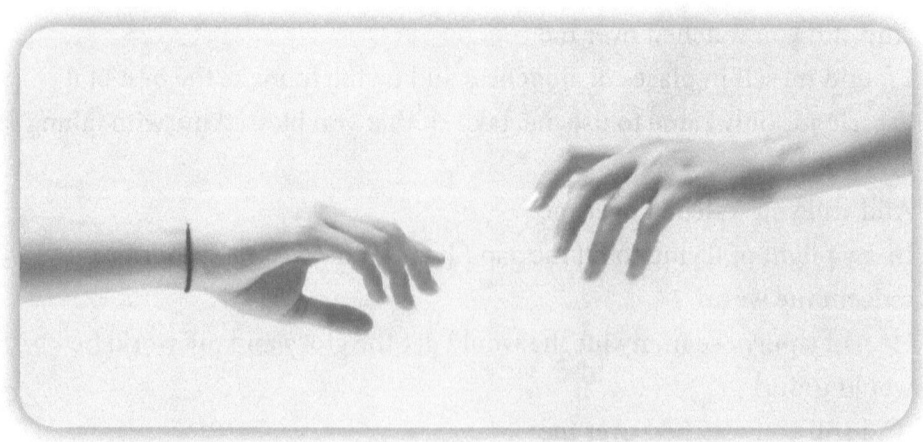

God's word is powerful. What does this scripture say to you?

_____

_____

_____

_____

_____

What have you learned during this time with Lord?

_____

_____

_____

_____

_____

Are there things you need to do differently?

_____

_____

_____

_____

_____

Before you leave this moment, write down God's directions to you.

_____

_____

_____

_____

_____

Close this journaling moment with a prayer.

_____

_____

_____

_____

_____

_____

Have I Ignored The Examples Of Baby Jesus?

Lord, you reduced your power to be contained in the birth of a baby boy
With the purpose to take on all experiences of man and to use his life to pay a debt of sin and destroy
As a young boy he separated himself to go to a place where people celebrated the Passover in the temple
He listened to the teaching going on and began to speak what his father wanted said the task was not simple

Often, we go to our churches and places of worship to share what the Lord has done for us
However, do we reach out to others and tell them about the Lord and that he is the one we trust
Do we take the time to share with someone that came to church that day/night because they needed a witness?
Someone to take the time to tell how the Lord, heals, restores and want to deliver us from so much stress

As Jesus grew, he did the work that his father sent him to do
He taught the words and encouraged others to become disciples reaching out to me and you
Today, we are called to disciple others to Christ, but first we must know that in his presence is joy
We must tell others of his word, his promises, how to watch and pray and stay away from Satan's ploy

At this point in our life are we about our father's work as Jesus did as a

12-year-old boy telling of God mercy and grace

Have we taken in enough word that our life speaks as the living word, or have we taken his word and let it go to waste?

All through the Bible we see Jesus in the body of man going through suffering, rejection, pain, yet giving God the Glory

This Christmas season look, for how you have handled the gift of son and how it has impacted our story

Remember all that he has given us, and asked for us to believe what he did for us is real.

Written as God helps me remember what Christmas was all about 12/3/2019,
© Dr. Cynthia Locke Henderson

God's word is powerful. What does this scripture say to you?

_____

_____

_____

_____

_____

What have you learned during this time with Lord?

_____

_____

_____

_____

_____

Are there things you need to do differently?

_____

_____

_____

_____

_____

Before you leave this moment, write down God's directions to you.

_____

_____

_____

_____

_____

Close this journaling moment with a prayer.

_____

_____

_____

_____

_____

Your Life Was Given Without A Price Tag, So Are Your Blessings

Great and marvelous are your deeds, Lord God Almighty. Just and
true are your ways, King of the nations.

(REVELATION 15:3)

Lord, no one gave a purchase order for the salvation you bring to me
My salvation can't be taxed to comply with the government demands, it
is free
Every day I wake from a rest where I sleep trusting that nothing would
occur
Lord, you kept the thief away, the harm away, I sleep in peace, thank you sir

Lord, when I wake, I breathe the air that gives life, I see my surroundings
No one can put a price tag on the days that you allow me to exist, you
king above all kings
Lord, it is the non-tangible tangible things that I sometime forget to tell
you how much you are appreciated
Lord, how excellent you are in all the world, you made me who I am
giving priceless gifts you never hesitated

Today, I have opportunity to read your word, pray and you listen, feel
your presence inside and outside
You don't hold it against me when I falter or fail you forgive me and
acknowledge that I tried
Great and marvelous are your works in my thoughts, in my safe passage
from days to days

Despite my imperfections, my forgetting to give you praise, You Lord are just and true in all your ways

Lord, the greatest gift you gave was the life of your only son
Lord, you gave us multiple sons and daughters and all you ask is we spiritually give them to you birthing is done
I don't know how I could handle it if someone took the life of my children, I would want them to pay
I have to release their life in your care, they came without a price tag, all you ask is that I train them your way

"You are worthy, our Lord and God, to receive glory and honor and power, for you created all things, and by your will they were created and have their being." (Revelation 4:11)

Lord, I worship you this season of celebrating your arrival to this earth!

Written as my heart flood with admiration of God gift to us, truly, Jesus is the reason for the season, 12/4/19 © Dr. Cynthia Locke Henderson

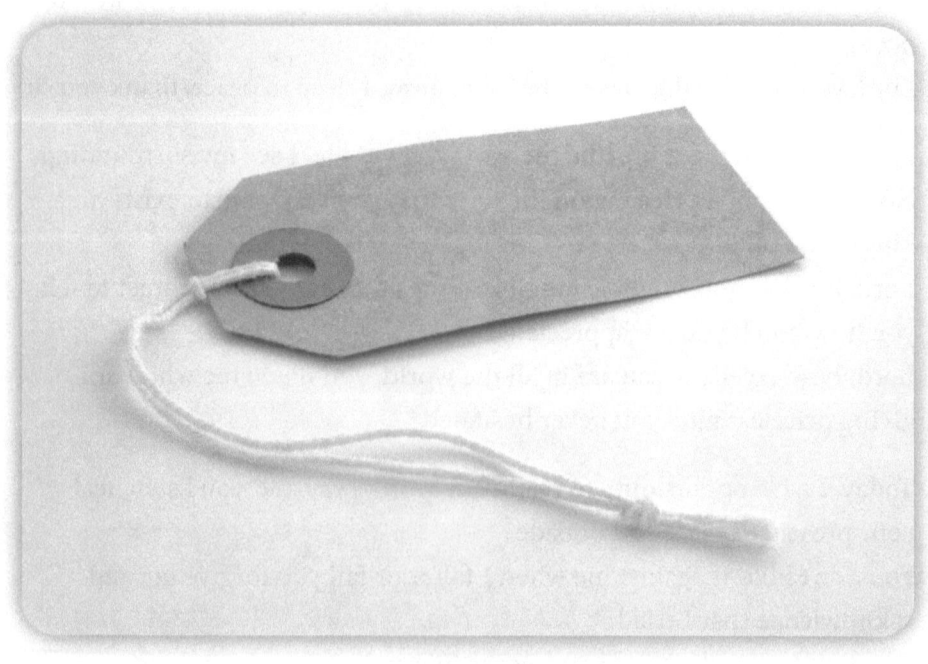

God's word is powerful. What does this scripture say to you?

_____

_____

_____

_____

_____

What have you learned during this time with Lord?

_____

_____

_____

_____

_____

Are there things you need to do differently?

_____

_____

_____

_____

_____

Before you leave this moment, write down God's directions to you.

_____

_____

_____

_____

_____

Close this journaling moment with a prayer.

_____

_____

_____

_____

_____

Jesus An Unimaginable Wonder

For God so loved the world that he gave his one and only Son, that
whoever believes in him shall not perish but have eternal life.

(JOHN 3:16)

This season we celebrate the birthday of a baby boy who was born
because of a commitment of love
It had to be love to give your only son, then reduce him in the form of
man and not a host from above
Some that don't understand would call him an illegitimate child
conceived in the womb of an unmarried mom
Believe me there was nothing illegitimate about him, the angel
announced his coming, he was a psalm

Psalms are sacred songs used to praise Deity, Baby Jesus was just that, he
psalms the works of God
This baby came as an example, a gift above any that we could ever imagine, he came as our rod
He embodied flesh like any other baby, he cried, he needed milk, he
needed to be swaddled and adored
He embodied flesh and felt all that man feels - the cold - born and laid in
a manger made from pieces of board

That manger was not just any piece of wood, it had purpose that we
never imagined or envisioned
To the animals his bed gave food; the hay and straw needed for them to
sustain and provide life's provision
To us that manger was like the most divine bed to ever exist, for it served

as the place for our savior's birth

Never see that manger as a prop to complete the story of a play, it was also a place that held of promises on earth

This little baby felt hunger so that he would know what it feels like to be empty inside and desire more

He brings salvation that allows us to remove all sin and begins to open every locked door

This little baby knew what it felt like to be loved by his mom first and then by a dad that did not give the seed of life

The same way this season is a celebration of God's love for us and desire that we not live in hatred and strife

***Because of all that God has done, I long to worship Him,
I was born to worship Him***

Inspired by the intricate steps that God took to define his love for us. Jesus is really the reason for the seasons of life. 12/5/19 © Dr. Cynthia Locke Henderson

God's word is powerful. What does this scripture say to you?

_____

_____

_____

_____

_____

What have you learned during this time with Lord?

_____

_____

_____

_____

_____

Are there things you need to do differently?

_____

_____

_____

_____

_____

Before you leave this moment, write down God's directions to you.

_____

_____

_____

_____

_____

Close this journaling moment with a prayer.

_____

_____

_____

_____

_____

The Gift That Keeps Giving

For the wages of sin is death, but the gift of God is eternal life
in Christ Jesus our Lord.

(ROMANS 6:23)

God gave mankind the gift of his son, when first unwrapped he was a baby boy
With a mission to come to us, see the sin in our life, pay the price for sin and destroy
God gave the greatest gift knowing that it would take a blood sacrifice and his death
To give us a chance to repent, and embody everlasting life that exceeds all wealth

This baby did not come with a pocket of gold and money to buy happiness, if only we realized he was God's son
This baby's entrance into this world was in some of the poorest accommodations in his nation
Despite an audience of farm animals that could not speak his language, God sent kings to worship him
His birth was announced before his conception, he was given his name by God and not a pseudonym

His resume preceded him, he was to be called Emanuel, meaning God is with us, giving us a chance for sin to cease
He will be called Wonderful Counselor, Mighty God, Everlasting Father, Prince of Peace.
This gift is still with us today, we have approval to go in the highway and

hedges and invite others to receive this gift

He came as a baby, lived to teach us God's word, died only to rise, He will return, don't miss this miraculous shift

This gift does not cost to share, share it, don't keep it to yourself

For God's gifts and his call are irrevocable. (Romans 11:29)

Written out of inspiration of a Baby Boy, a gift of God on 12/6/2019
© Dr. Cynthia Locke Henderson

God's word is powerful. What does this scripture say to you?

_____

_____

_____

_____

_____

What have you learned during this time with Lord?

_____

_____

_____

_____

_____

Are there things you need to do differently?

_____

_____

_____

_____

_____

Before you leave this moment, write down God's directions to you.

_____

_____

_____

_____

_____

Close this journaling moment with a prayer.

_____

_____

_____

_____

_____

_____

Be It Unto Me

"I am the Lord's servant," Mary answered. "May your word to me be fulfilled." Then the angel left her.

(LUKE 1:38)

Lord, you know my name,
You know who I am going to be,
You know the places I have been
You know where I will go in life,
You know what I will do,
You have the road map for my trip

With all that knowledge, you let me make decisions
Even when my choices may feel like they are not the right ones
You allow me to advance forward and follow my heart
You let me feel the consequences of my choice
You allow me to fall, but you leave room and time for me to get up
You are not a slave master you give me free will

Just as the angel went to Mary and announced the birth of Jesus
She willingly accepted and said "May it be unto me according to your word"
Lord, you give us your word in the Bible, in sermons, in revivals,
You speak through others; you speak directly to us in our hearts
You warn us time after time, experience after experience,
Then Lord you give us opportunity after opportunity and allow me to walk through open doors

This year of celebrating your birth, help us to be willing like Mary
Help us to accept your birth in our lives and say, be it unto us,
Help us be willing to take your directions because you have already done the hard part

216

You became like us and dwelt among us, you took the ridicule, you took pain in your flesh and heart
You walked many roads - proving your love, healing sick and demonstrating the miraculous love and power of God
Your final act made it known, that you were born to die for us, Lord be birth in my thoughts, my ways, my life

Your will for me, I say as Mary said, Be it unto me

Written as God Continues to show me the real reason for the season.
©12/9/19, Dr. Cynthia Locke Henderson©

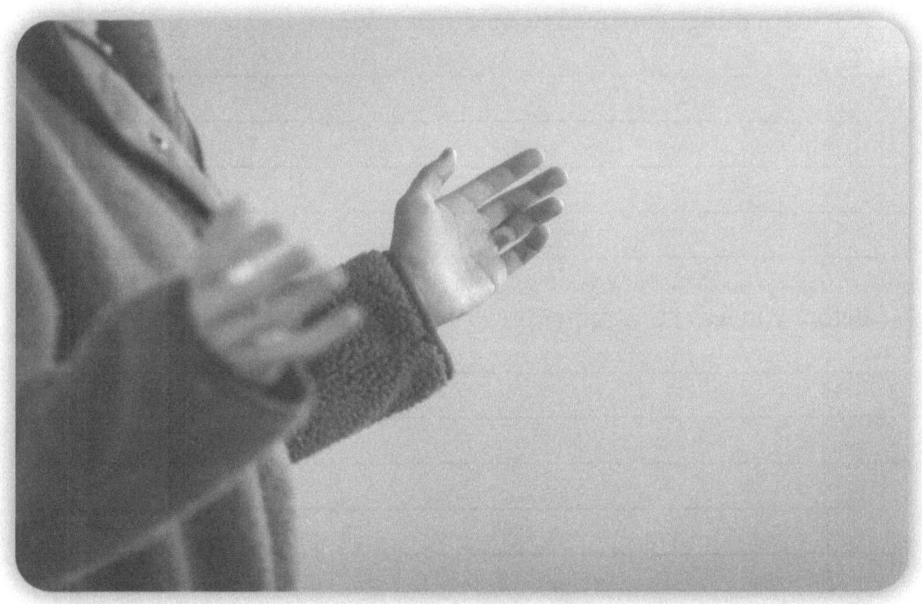

God's word is powerful. What does this scripture say to you?

_____

_____

_____

_____

_____

What have you learned during this time with Lord?

_____

_____

_____

_____

_____

Are there things you need to do differently?

_____

_____

_____

_____

_____

Before you leave this moment, write down God's directions to you.

_____

_____

_____

_____

_____

Close this journaling moment with a prayer.

_____

_____

_____

_____

_____

The Gift We Really Need Is Not Under The Tree

For unto us a child is born, unto us a son is given: and
the government shall be upon his shoulder: and his name
shall be called Wonderful, Counselor, The mighty God,
The everlasting Father, The Prince of Peace.

(ISAIAH 9:6 KJV)

When I was a child, I desired gifts wrapped in wrapping paper gold, silver and red
On the day we celebrate your birthday as a child I could hardly wait to get out of my bed
Sugar plums and candy did not dance about in my head, I simply wondered if I would get a doll with hair
A tea set, a doll house, a pretty new dress, new socks, I knew there would be fruit and at least a pear

Now that I am grown and understand your word more, I know what I need and want more of that baby who became a man
I want to understand more that Emanuel means God is with us, whatever life brings our way, or what is in our plan
I have learned that in times like these, the government's demands are sometimes unbearable and creates many snares
I realized my gift was not under that tree but in a manger, made from a tree and continues to be present, He cares

I wondered what it felt like to have a father, wondering if there was a special feeling I had missed, I wanted one
Repeatedly, this baby took the role of the father that I missed, frequently calming my fears when all else was done

This year I am not anxiously waiting for the gift wrapped in red and gold craftly wrapped laying under the tree

This Christmas I want that gift that was called Everlasting Father, Prince of peace, Counselor, I want Him in me

Happy Birthday Jesus. Thank you for being my gift wrapped in swaddling clothes.

Written as inspired by God in celebration of the birth of Jesus and real reason for the season. © 12/10/2019 Dr. Cynthia L Henderson

God's word is powerful. What does this scripture say to you?

_____

_____

_____

_____

_____

What have you learned during this time with Lord?

_____

_____

_____

_____

_____

Are there things you need to do differently?

_____

_____

_____

_____

_____

Before you leave this moment, write down God's directions to you.

_____

_____

_____

_____

_____

Close this journaling moment with a prayer.

_____

_____

_____

_____

_____

_____

Transitioned For Us

Today in the town of David a Savior has been born to you;
he is the Messiah, the Lord.

(PSALM 91:2)

God, you went through a transition just for us and did not short cut
any of your plan
You followed order to help us understand the details of your love for man
Born a baby that would come in the most humblest form, laid in simplify
You came blameless, sinless, without intervention to cause your birth,
just holy authenticity,
Baby with purpose
You gave your earthly parents just a little time to parent you because you
had purpose and things to do
You taught in the temple, the heart of where men would go for life's
directions and the pursuit of what was true
You taught the word and will of your father, and then you replicated
your will in the disciples to train to do as you did
Surely you went many places, raised your friend from the dead, fed
thousands who listened to things to forbid
Man with a mission
Despite all the good that you brought to this world, the sacrifices you
endured to give words of significance
You did not waiver, nor give up your mission, some betrayed you and
slept as you prayed but you took a firm stance
Endured man's rejection and accusation that you were not the king of
this world where you wanted man free
Then you gave the ultimate sacrifice of your life through a bludgeoning
death on a tree

On wood you were laid as a baby and on wood you were laid as man
And from those pieces of wood your body was removed and placed in a
tomb, following God's plan
And three days later you rose from all the fragilities of mankind
You rose our Savior and none like any can find, yes you are no longer
baby, man, you have a Holy redesign Savior

Written as I am understanding how Jesus is the real reason for the season.
12/11/19 Dr. Cynthia l. Henderson

✎ God's word is powerful. What does this scripture say to you?

_____
_____
_____
_____
_____

✎ What have you learned during this time with Lord?

_____
_____
_____
_____
_____

✎ Are there things you need to do differently?

_____
_____
_____
_____
_____

✎ Before you leave this moment, write down God's directions to you.

_____
_____
_____
_____
_____

✎ Close this journaling moment with a prayer.

_____
_____
_____
_____
_____

How Excellent Is Your Name In All The Earth

To the Chief Musician. On the instrument of Gath. A Psalm of David.
O LORD, our Lord, how excellent is Your name in all the earth,
Who have set Your glory above the heavens!

(Psalm 8:1 NKJV)

Lord, this season I contemplate your excellence in the gift you gave to this world
I think of how you in the heavens hurled plants, the moon, sun and on that night in the sky a special star was hurled
A star that led others to witness the birth of baby Jesus, powerful then and still powerful and making impact
Many gifts will be given on your birthday celebration, yet none can compare with your gift that is a standing fact

You thought of it all, the good, bad, evil and what we would do with the blessing that you gave
Despite all that lied ahead, the hatred, the killings, the shootings of children, this world you wanted to save
Despite the babies that die in infant mortality, poverty, discrimination, abandonment, incurable disease

God you chose to come to us in the form of a baby that would endure all that man's corruption would breed
Lord, this baby grew to be a man and gave us his sweat, blood, his life on calvary's hill
So that we would have forgiveness, healing, peace, be mercy giving, love giving and freedom to do your will

When we look back, I can't help but wonder what more, how much more, my God why are we taking so long
To realize the birth, the teachings of Jesus, his walk on the earth, his sacrifices to right our inside and outside wrongs

We have to wake up before we are completely lost
Forgetting the real reason for the season and how much this birthday celebration had to cost

Written as inspired by God to help me understand all that is included in this Birthday Celebration on 12/ 12/2019 © Dr. Cynthia Locke Henderson

God's word is powerful. What does this scripture say to you?

_____

_____

_____

_____

_____

What have you learned during this time with Lord?

_____

_____

_____

_____

_____

Are there things you need to do differently?

_____

_____

_____

_____

_____

Before you leave this moment, write down God's directions to you.

_____

_____

_____

_____

_____

Close this journaling moment with a prayer.

_____

_____

_____

_____

_____

Thanks For Making Me, Me

I am the vine; you are the branches. If you remain in me
and I in you, you will bear much fruit; apart from me
you can do nothing

(JOHN 15:5)

Lord, thank you that I was not in charge in the creation of me
I would have focused on perfection, beauty, everything my heart desired
to be
I would have left a few empty spaces and holes that I could not fill
I would have wasted so much and not been able to cover the cost of the bill

You are the vine, my source, and I am a simple branch, without you I am
nothing unless connected to the source
I come empty without any directions on how I should navigate through
this tremendous life course
I think about you in the form of a baby boy, named before you arrived,
not asking for specific accommodations
An angel announced his coming to Mary, she did not decide boy or girl,
she just knew that he would save a nation

You gave him what was needed to overcome the sins in your other
creations, mankind, humans, never satisfied, "US"
God, you put us in the hands of this baby, despite all that ensued, his
response - Father thy will be done without a fuss
I know you created us to worship you, but life happened, life tried to fill
empty spaces and fill in holes
That's why I am glad you created me, your will and purpose for me was
in the life of this baby who would rescue many souls

Thank you for making me, me. You knew I needed your reinforcement

However, as it is written: "What no eye has seen, what no ear has heard, and what no human mind has conceived" – the things God has prepared for those who love him— (1 Corinthians 2:9)

Written because God made me the way that I am 12/13/2019 © Dr. Cynthia L. Henderson

God's word is powerful. What does this scripture say to you?

_____
_____
_____
_____
_____

What have you learned during this time with Lord?

_____
_____
_____
_____
_____

Are there things you need to do differently?

_____
_____
_____
_____
_____

Before you leave this moment, write down God's directions to you.

_____
_____
_____
_____
_____

Close this journaling moment with a prayer.

_____
_____
_____
_____
_____

I Saw You,
When You Did Not See Me

For I know the plans I have for you", declares the LORD, "plans to prosper you and not to harm you, plans to give you hope and a future."

(JEREMIAH 29:11)

I had no idea that you were placed in my life cycle for a reason
I could only be deeply amazed because you stayed there not just one, but many seasons
You have been there through your highs, my lows and your families limitless
You have withstood everything life has thrown your way you give it your best

There are countless times, I felt like we asked so much of you
You stood still, treated us with your care and continued to do all the wonderful things that you do
I have never seen you claim the Christian label
But when I see all that God has placed on you in and out of your trials, He is always at your table

Sometimes I wonder if God is listening to me when I pray, I wonder if he will give me my desire
Just when I think God did not hear me, he uses you to bless me and takes my worship higher
I am not replacing you as my God, I am thanking God because He sent you to do his deed
Sometimes it takes time before he brings it to pass, then other times you show up at record speed

I need you to know that you have not gone un-noticed by God and certainly not by me
You are that person that had withstood, thunderstorms, tsunamis, and still you stand as a strong tree
None of us knew why God put you in the midst of roads that were taking us places God wanted us to go
He had plans to give us hope and a future, he knew what he wanted us to know

You are what God gave us for Christmas wrapped up in a tremendous wrapping of care, love and sacrifice
What he did for this world, for your sins, my sins, no man can set a value or a price
God announced the blessing of a baby king to the world and his servant Mary
But you Rashard, God sent you a baby, a boy, a man to your mother Carrie

Your love for us, your family has been silent, quietly flowing through your hearts
It has been there seemly un-noticed from the beginning of your life, from the various starts
God has been working all things together for your good Rashard, he has a predestined purpose for you
Continue in the care, love and sacrifice that you feel in your heart, just do what you do

And we know that in all things God works for the good of those who love him, who have been called according to his purpose. (Romans 8:28)

Written as God put words to your mother-in-law's thoughts, prayers and to her heart on December 14, 2019 Collaboration of Diann McCall and Dr. Cynthia Locke Henderson

God's word is powerful. What does this scripture say to you?

_____

_____

_____

_____

_____

What have you learned during this time with Lord?

_____

_____

_____

_____

_____

Are there things you need to do differently?

_____

_____

_____

_____

_____

Before you leave this moment, write down God's directions to you.

_____

_____

_____

_____

_____

Close this journaling moment with a prayer.

_____

_____

_____

_____

_____

_____

Unforgiveness Attempted To Stop Baby Jesus' Birth Plans

The LORD saw how great the wickedness of the human race had become on the earth, and that every inclination of the thoughts of the human heart was only evil all the time. The LORD regretted that he had made human beings on the earth, and his heart was deeply troubled. So, the LORD said, "I will wipe from the face of the earth the human race I have created--and with them the animals, the birds and the creatures that move along the ground--for I regret that I have made them."

(GENESIS 6: 5-7)

The world was full of wickedness and controlled by mankind's law in an effort to cause order
Having a baby without a husband was seen as evil, against the law, but what God saw was much broader
This law distressed Joseph who had desired Mary the virgin to be his wife
With the evil in the world at that time Joseph felt he had selected a way free of the evil, free of the world's strife

Then the turning point occurred, and unforgiveness no longer had a place in the heart of Joseph the appointed man
Unforgiveness would have caused him to turn his back on Mary because of personal belief and law was against his plan
He forgave Mary in his heart for when he thought a wrongness has occurred
The turning point occurred because they both believed on the word of God and what the angel said, they heard

In the beginning God created the world, man and all that existed sealing it with a statement that "It is good"

Animals on the earth, green plants were on the ground for food, men and women, everything was where it should

So, God demonstrated forgiveness of mankind and all of his evilness, and regretted that he had created us

He sent his only son for our salvation through an enormous path of forgiveness only asking us to believe and trust

"For God did not send his Son into the world to condemn the world, but in order that the world might be saved through him. Whoever believes in him is not condemned, but whoever does not believe is condemned already, because he has not believed in the name of the only Son of God." (John 3:17–18 ESV)

God forgave, what is stopping us?

Written as deeply inspired by God alone and as he ordered on 12/16/2019
© *Dr. Cynthia Locke. Henderson*

(/) God's word is powerful. What does this scripture say to you?

_____
_____
_____
_____
_____

(/) What have you learned during this time with Lord?

_____
_____
_____
_____
_____

(/) Are there things you need to do differently?

_____
_____
_____
_____
_____

(/) Before you leave this moment, write down God's directions to you.

_____
_____
_____
_____
_____

(/) Close this journaling moment with a prayer.

_____
_____
_____
_____
_____

Jesus' Birth Demonstrated Lessons In Obedience

"I am the Lord's servant," Mary answered. "May your word to me be fulfilled." Then the angel left her.

(LUKE 1:38)

Gabriel told Mary she would be the mother of God's son, no other women would be his earthly mother, no never
You will have this baby who is destined for greatness, destined to be king over a kingdom that will be forever
Mary's first response was of an earthly mindset, which says this can't happen to me, I have been with no one
As the angel Gabriel continued giving her a message from God, she said, "I am the Lord's servant, let all said be done"

Mary was not the only one to respond in obedience with the prerequisites of the baby Jesus' birth
The shepherds, quit their jobs, listened and then followed the directions - taken the angel's word at its worth
They did not give the excuse we give telling the Lord, not today, but tomorrow, I give myself tomorrow
Not realizing tomorrow may be too late, disobedience can bring tragedy and tragedy can bring sorrow

After Jesus's birth, the Maji better known as wise men, some call them kings, came looking for the king
Herod desired to kill the king, but the Magi followed the prophesy and wanted to worship the king and bring offering
Repeatedly his said, that the government, the weight of the world will be

on his shoulder, still he will be our Savior

Be obedient to reason for this season, don't say, tomorrow, I give myself tomorrow and take a salvation waiver

How many times will you get a chance to respond to the reason for the season!

Written as I really begin to understand the reason for the season on 12/17/2019

© Dr. Cynthia Locke. Henderson

God's word is powerful. What does this scripture say to you?

_____

_____

_____

_____

_____

What have you learned during this time with Lord?

_____

_____

_____

_____

_____

Are there things you need to do differently?

_____

_____

_____

_____

_____

Before you leave this moment, write down God's directions to you.

_____

_____

_____

_____

_____

Close this journaling moment with a prayer.

_____

_____

_____

_____

_____

_____

Unto Us A Son Is Given

For God so loved the world that he gave his one and only Son, that whoever believes in him shall not perish but have eternal life.

(JOHN 3:16)

Jesus was a son given because God planned life for us without selection of a son through adoption
God knew what state the world was in and he wanted us to have an option
This world was headed on a rapid road to damnation without salvation and a Savior
For only God could address the sinful and evil behavior

He found in Mary purity and a servant who was willingEven today he seeks those who want and believe him, because salvation he's freely givingSacrifices were necessary for establishing a covenant, so God continued the order by sacrificing his son
The impact of sin caused each one of us to be born in sin and shaped in inequity because of what man had done

In the beginning was the word, the word was with God and the word was God, a perfect trinity relationship
He created man and gave him a mate, so he created a relationship that was the next part of the creation script
An act of love he created another perfect relationship, but man destroyed it and sin entered causing life to be grim
God did not stop loving, he gave us his son so that this time we would have a chance for a life everlasting with him

He gave his son to prevent a death without repentance, how much more does he have to do to prove his love for us

This baby born came innocently, suffered innocently, and died innocently so that we could believe and trust

Time is running out, earth is destroying itself, how many more
Christmas celebrations must we have to honor God's gift

Not tomorrow, today, now, not the next Christmas celebration, must we
decide to take the salvation shift

God has waited for us to get it together. Why are we wasting time?

*Written as I really begin to understand the reason for the season on 12/18/2019 © Dr.
Cynthia Locke. Henderson*

✏ God's word is powerful. What does this scripture say to you?

_____
_____
_____
_____
_____

✏ What have you learned during this time with Lord?

_____
_____
_____
_____
_____

✏ Are there things you need to do differently?

_____
_____
_____
_____
_____

✏ Before you leave this moment, write down God's directions to you.

_____
_____
_____
_____
_____

✏ Close this journaling moment with a prayer.

_____
_____
_____
_____
_____

Born To Know Us Inside And Out

Do not conform to the pattern of this world, but be transformed by the renewing of your mind. Then you will be able to test and approve what God's will is--his good, pleasing and perfect will.

(ROMANS 12:2)

Jesus came to this earth in the lowest form of a human - a baby
From the time of his announcement there were no intended second thoughts or a maybe
He was coming in flesh like you and I with all the things we needed when born in our special room
A place to be born, a place to lay after his mom had finished her job of carrying him in her womb

A baby destined to be the Prince of Peace, how would he stop the world he came into and cause chaos and sin to cease
He was born with the threat of others wanting to take his life so that his time to be king would decease
Things are happening or have occurred that literally purpose to take our life and bring God's plans for us to a halt
Attacks on our health, our self-esteem, our relationships, our desire to live, death of loved ones and things not our fault

Jesus came for such a time as this, his life is a pattern for how we respond to life's disappointments and threats
His life is really terminated and eradicate sin in our life because he was born to cancel not some but all of our debt
All he asks is for us to believe and accept him as our gift of salvation, not

the one that is temporary and under the tree

Imagine our baby Jesus born with purpose is available, are you available to receive salvation and live a life that is free

Can I stand to be free of things that block my destiny with the Lord? NO!

Written as I continue to really see Jesus as the only reason for the season on 12/19/2019

© Dr. Cynthia Locke. Henderson

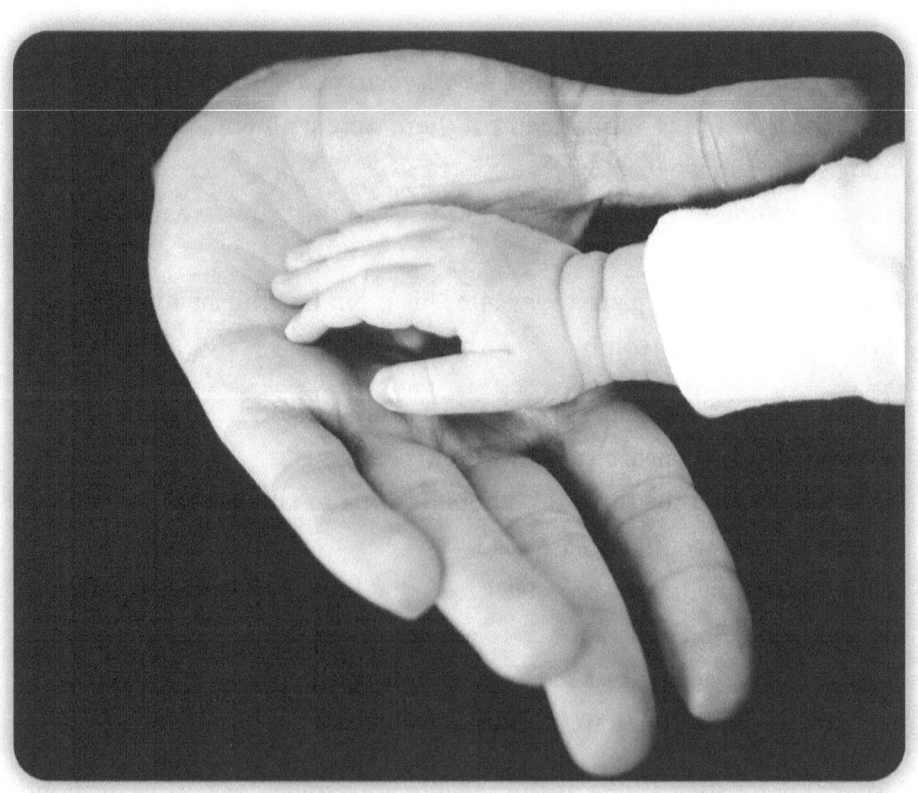

God's word is powerful. What does this scripture say to you?

_____

_____

_____

_____

_____

What have you learned during this time with Lord?

_____

_____

_____

_____

_____

Are there things you need to do differently?

_____

_____

_____

_____

_____

Before you leave this moment, write down God's directions to you.

_____

_____

_____

_____

_____

Close this journaling moment with a prayer.

_____

_____

_____

_____

_____

_____

Don't Leave Your Gift Under The Tree

"Behold, the virgin shall be with child, and bear a Son, and they shall call His name Immanuel," which is translated, "God with us."

(MATTHEW 1:23 NKJV)

We have gone in the malls and searched for the best price for our gifts
We picked things that would give us or our loved ones the happy lift of lifts
The tree looks better now with the colorful decorations and the glowing and blinking lights
Everything for the celebration and the birthday of someone else that represented the epitome of what is right

In two days, the presents will be unwrapped, the paper recycled, the boxes and tags all trashed
The surprise element gone, some regrets that we did not get the one gift we wanted, that idea has been trashed
The only thing left under the tree was the understanding that Jesus is the reason for this season
It is then that we feel as though we have committed a birthday celebration treason

There is still time for us to take a moment and realize that God is with us and has been there since his birth
He gave the gift of salvation, priceless, wrapped in honor and willing to give salvation to everyone on this earth
Don't forget that last present that is an omniscient, omnipresent, omnipotent, Immanuel the baby boy

The government will be on his shoulder, he will be our Savior, our rock, our provider, our strength our everlasting joy

May I never forget the real reason for this season; may it teach me to give and give his words for that is where life lives.

Written as God really helped me focus on the reason for the season. 12/23/19
© *Dr. Cynthia Locke. Henderson*

God's word is powerful. What does this scripture say to you?

_____

_____

_____

_____

_____

What have you learned during this time with Lord?

_____

_____

_____

_____

_____

Are there things you need to do differently?

_____

_____

_____

_____

_____

Before you leave this moment, write down God's directions to you.

_____

_____

_____

_____

_____

Close this journaling moment with a prayer.

_____

_____

_____

_____

_____

_____

He Came Because Of Love

But he was pierced for our transgressions, he was crushed for our iniquities; the punishment that brought us peace was on him, and by his wounds we are healed.

(ISAIAH 53:5)

It was the night before Jesus was born and there were no guest room for his mother to complete this pregnancy
Yet he had to be born, this was the only way to give us a remedy for sin, Mary needed a place for this expectancy
A place where animals were given nourishment and water became an alternate location for this baby's bed
In that same place where animals were fed, Jesus now laid in swaddling clothes, he was the source for man to be fed

He survived the slaughtering of baby boys by King Herod's resolve to destroy the Messiah, our Savior and King
His family traveled to Bethlehem to register and honor the laws of the land first, then his mission of salvation to bring
For a world that was currently in chaos and full of sin bound for a future of sinfulness without redemption
God loved us so much that he allowed this baby boy to begin a path bringing salvation to all without any exemptions

Given all that you and I have gone through in life, how much we have been given, when we did not deserve grace
How often have we backslid, did the wrong thing, yet our Jesus loved and our sins were forgiven and erased
Remember this night before the big celebration what it took to bring us this far, to love despite of our sins and mistakes

There he laid in a manger wrapped in swaddling clothes a gift sent because of love preparing for our iniquities to take

Imagine his birthday cake with millions of candles representing generations of boys, girls, women and men,
Imagine icing covering the holes, dips, the cracks in the cake below, yet all he sees is his covering minus flaw and sin
Imagine his blowing out the candles to stop the flames from destroying the millions of candles, each a unique candle
Imagine Jesus saying I'll keep my candles, I will know each one, if they believe, their life I can handle

It is not your birthday; thank him for the gift and make room for him, he was the Birthday boy

Written as I learn to celebrate Baby Jesus' Birthday on 12/24/19
© Dr. Cynthia Locke. Henderson

God's word is powerful. What does this scripture say to you?

_____

_____

_____

_____

_____

What have you learned during this time with Lord?

_____

_____

_____

_____

_____

Are there things you need to do differently?

_____

_____

_____

_____

_____

Before you leave this moment, write down God's directions to you.

_____

_____

_____

_____

_____

Close this journaling moment with a prayer.

_____

_____

_____

_____

_____

_____

From Human To Divine

For God so loved the world that he gave his one and only Son, that whoever believes in him shall not perish but have eternal life.

(JOHN 3:16)

From an immaculate birth your existence into mankind began
Your father was up to remedying the destruction and sin on his created land
Everything he created was intended to be good
But the man he created first did not do as he should

God created woman from the flesh of man's flesh and bone of man's bone
This time through a spotless, perfect and clean conception he gave his son who shared the rights to the throne
He allowed him to feel the intensity and inclusiveness of all that a human could feel
He did not have think about what we feel, God allowed his son to experience what was real

He sent him for the ones that think they have not been loved enough
Despite all that humans have in their possession all valuable, all state of the art, all sorts of stuff
He allowed this baby, his son, the great I am to have all and see it amount to nothing
And from that pile of nothing, only that baby could make nothing become much as it was touched by our King

To the one who felt I have been treated wrong and live a life under dark cloud after dark cloud
To that one that has felt he has always walked in the rear of those who enjoy the successful crowd

God has and continues to provide; he continues to give strength through his word

He continues to say I love you; I am with you always; I am your God until all of his care transferred

We celebrate because as humans, your bore our pain, felt our shame, our rejection, our death

You became a human and took on a bill that we created and paid the cost out of your holy wealth

This day celebrated as the day you were born, the greatest, most immaculate originated baby boy

You gave us the honor and privilege to endure all that humans endure, and yet feel you inhabit us with eternal joy

Oh, that I never forget that everything I feel, you felt it also

Everything that I need for eternal life, you make sure I know

You made a shift from human to divine transitioning through tremendous pain on calvary

May I never, never, forget Lord that you did it all for a sinner like me

Happy Birthday JESUS

"He himself bore our sins" in his body on the cross, so that we might die to sins and live for righteousness; "by his wounds you have been healed." (1 Peter 2:24)

Written on your birthday celebration with such intense feelings of your presence during my alone time 12/25/19 © Dr. Cynthia Locke. Henderson

God's word is powerful. What does this scripture say to you?

_____
_____
_____
_____
_____

What have you learned during this time with Lord?

_____
_____
_____
_____
_____

Are there things you need to do differently?

_____
_____
_____
_____
_____

Before you leave this moment, write down God's directions to you.

_____
_____
_____
_____
_____

Close this journaling moment with a prayer.

_____
_____
_____
_____
_____

The Party Is Over And You Are Still Giving

Therefore, since we have a great high priest who has ascended into heaven, Jesus the Son of God, let us hold firmly to the faith we profess.

(HEBREWS 4:14)

Yesterday, we celebrated your birth with lights, presents, candles, stars, and trees
We garnished our spaces with favorite foods and candies, your gift was not one of these
Yet we heard sermons that let us know we were able to give gifts because you taught us to give
More importantly you taught us that when all the celebration has concluded, for you we absolutely must live

The same wrong in this world that required your father to give you as a sacrifice to remedy our immorality and sin
We must be sober, vigilant and ever seeking your will because the devil is seeking whom he may devour and win
It is now that we must turn our eyes and heart on Jesus, and never let him go, never forget that he's still giving
He is still forgiving, offering life giving resources, and supporting us with grace and mercy for righteous living

He is still giving peace when the world seems to crumble around you and man or women continues to disappoint you
He is there unchanging, willing to make your little much, willing to never forsake and strength for the things you pursue
He is not the relationship that leaves before or after the celebration, he is committed to the plans he has for us

He is a discerner of thoughts and intents of our hearts. He grants our wants and wishes as we give him our trust

Lord you are incredibly amazing, you are worthy of my praise in all that lies ahead, good are bad
The party is over, but you are still here, thank you Lord,
my master, my king

Written during my time alone with God as he reassured me of his commitment to me
12/26/19 © Dr. Cynthia Locke. Henderson

Lord you are my sunshine at the break of day and after the rain clouds of life,

God's word is powerful. What does this scripture say to you?

_____
_____
_____
_____
_____

What have you learned during this time with Lord?

_____
_____
_____
_____
_____

Are there things you need to do differently?

_____
_____
_____
_____
_____

Before you leave this moment, write down God's directions to you.

_____
_____
_____
_____
_____

Close this journaling moment with a prayer.

_____
_____
_____
_____
_____

Lord You Are Consistent

Trust in the LORD with all your heart and lean not on your own understanding.

(PROVERBS 3:5)

Lord, nothing in our personal life remains the same, somedays up and somedays down
Something sad for what is done by others can cause a shift in our confidence and turn us around
Sometimes things done by others can cause a tsunami of feelings that shift everything we thought we had overcome
Our inconsistency of trust seems to move us in a place we don't want to admit that we come from

You are so patient yet a true teacher of the heart who allows us to go through the feeling lessons again and again
We cry silent tears and try to hide what's going on inside, wondering why Lord have I found myself again, with this pain
We find ourselves on the cliff of wondering if it will ever go away, then you Lord reach inside and rescue from our self
You step into our depression, loneliness, insufficiency, hopelessness, dejection, and feeling that nothing good is left

You Lord are consistent, the same yesterday and today, time and time again, unchanging and especially fair
Thank you for bringing your words to our memory, your commitment to reach in response to a simple prayer
Each time you teach us lessons about feelings, I feel myself finally getting it, decreasing the blow that feelings transport
I have to be consistent with trusting God and telling unholy feelings, cease to strive, abort, I trust God, abort, abort

Commit your way to the LORD; trust in him and he will do this:
(Psalm 37:5)

"Come to me, all you who are weary and burdened, and I will give you rest. Matthew 11: 28

In the midst of everything drying up around me, is the promise of life, still growing, within me. 12/28/19 © Dr. Cynthia Locke. Henderson

/ God's word is powerful. What does this scripture say to you?

_____

_____

_____

_____

_____

/ What have you learned during this time with Lord?

_____

_____

_____

_____

_____

/ Are there things you need to do differently?

_____

_____

_____

_____

_____

/ Before you leave this moment, write down God's directions to you.

_____

_____

_____

_____

_____

/ Close this journaling moment with a prayer.

_____

_____

_____

_____

_____

"Keep Me Looking Up And Moving Forward!"

I lift up my eyes to the mountains-- where does my help come from?
My help comes from the LORD, the Maker of heaven and earth.

(PSALM 121:1-2)

Lord, thank you for arming me with an upward mentality, despite all that was down
Thank you for awakening me and understanding that it is time to move forward towards earning my life crown
There is a lot of work that needs to be done, I have learned so much as I reviewed past experiences and trials
I've gone many miles, endured growing pains learned lessons intended for me, now it's time to move to the next miles

I have not done anything to get me to this place I find myself in, it was your hand of grace, mercy, and abundance
All I can do at this moment is say THANK YOU, it makes me want to look to you and dance like David danced
Thank you for letting me leave the past in the past and now reaching for new revelations and new directions
Lord, I choose to listen to your calling, I choose to move past reflections, it is a new day and I move at your selections

Lord, my souls feels as if it is exploding with anticipation and small amounts of limitations
I am still in human flesh, but knowing that the rest of the journey is being designed by your spiritual foundations
I lift my head and look to you, that is where my strength comes from,

you are my source and I am ready for the course

Please keep me looking up and moving forward, there is none like you, for you are my guiding force

Oh, may the rivers of life that flow through my body at this moment, keep flowing!

Then Asa called to the LORD his God and said, "LORD, there is no one like you to help the powerless against the mighty. Help us, LORD our God, for we rely on you, and in your name, we have come against this vast army (of life). LORD, you are our God; do not let mere mortals prevail against you." (2 Chronicles 14:11)

Written as God inspired me and as I celebrated the ending of a year on 12/30/19 © Dr. Cynthia Locke. Henderson

✏ God's word is powerful. What does this scripture say to you?

_____
_____
_____
_____
_____

✏ What have you learned during this time with Lord?

_____
_____
_____
_____
_____

✏ Are there things you need to do differently?

_____
_____
_____
_____
_____

✏ Before you leave this moment, write down God's directions to you.

_____
_____
_____
_____
_____

✏ Close this journaling moment with a prayer.

_____
_____
_____
_____
_____
_____

I Am Nothing Without You

Through him all things were made; without him nothing was made
that has been made.

(JOHN 1:3)

Lord, I awake this morning and I am nothing without you in my life
physically and mentally
Without you how would the air know how to travel through my body
strategically
I could not direct my heart to beat in time with all the other orchestrations that I have in my being
I cannot create a brain and tell it what to tell me or teach it how to navigate my seeing

You see I yield myself to you with gratitude for every moveable part of me
I walk to the various part of this place called my home where I can
praise you and be free
You give me the freedom to choose you are to choose the world and
chaos, destruction and obliteration
Lord man has difficulty being free with you and hindered by not knowing that you are the author of creation

That is why, this day I thank you for a mind that worships you because
you have proven that you are my Savior
Lord, I acknowledge that all that I am and will ever be is because I am
your heir and you give me favor
The blessing in what you are to me often feels unique, however I know
with assurance that your offers are to all
It is not a mistake that I want to be available, I want to answer when you
call

I do not give in to the little aches and pain that make me not want to move because of the pain

Then I remembered the stories, pictures of the blood that you shed on calvary, I cannot forget the stain

The stain of your conclusion as man and experiencing everything that life has thrown my way

I realize that I am because you are, I am invited to be loved and to serve you on this day

I am nothing without you, thanks for letting me be yours!

Now the Lord is the Spirit, and where the Spirit of the Lord is, there is freedom. (2 Corinthians 3:17)

Written as I realized that I am just the pile of dirt created in the Master's hand at the end of this year 12/31/2019, © Dr Cynthia Locke Henderson

God's word is powerful. What does this scripture say to you?

_____

_____

_____

_____

_____

What have you learned during this time with Lord?

_____

_____

_____

_____

_____

Are there things you need to do differently?

_____

_____

_____

_____

_____

Before you leave this moment, write down God's directions to you.

_____

_____

_____

_____

_____

Close this journaling moment with a prayer.

_____

_____

_____

_____

_____

New Year, New Chance To Make Different Decisions

You will seek me and find me when you seek me with all your heart.

(JEREMIAH 29:13)

Lord, this is another year to do less of behaviors that rob me from being the person available to you
You already know what is in my heart and what should not be there, so to you I want to be completely true
You do not put stipulations on me, instead with arms wide open, you asked that I come just as I am
I have to trust you to guide me, because I have work to do. You have set my destiny and program

Too long I have relied on my thoughts and programs, when I know that you have my plans and interests in your heart
Lord, you have matured me to listen, pray more, build a strong relationship with you, for my new start
Everything in the past has its place in your plan for me even the good and the bad, it all groomed me for this year
Every year I get new glasses to see better, so this year, I see the plans you have to prosper me to see "spiritually clear"

To be carnally minded is death, but to increase my vision with a spiritual mindset and clarity is life and peace
I need to seek you more to rid myself of broken pieces as you cause my attractions to distractions to cease
Lord, I walk into this new year, knowing that you are where you have always been for me, that is AVAILABLE

Lord, you have put plans in my life that are accessible, help me reach them because I know they are OBTAINABLE

This is not just a new year; it is chance to walk in the freedom and liberty of the Lord.

For I know the plans I have for you," declares the LORD, "plans to prosper you and not to harm you, plans to give you hope and a future. (Jeremiah 29:11)

Written as inspired by God while in his presence at the same place where we meet.
1/1/2020 © Dr. Cynthia Locke Henderson

God's word is powerful. What does this scripture say to you?

_____
_____
_____
_____
_____

What have you learned during this time with Lord?

_____
_____
_____
_____
_____

Are there things you need to do differently?

_____
_____
_____
_____
_____

Before you leave this moment, write down God's directions to you.

_____
_____
_____
_____
_____

Close this journaling moment with a prayer.

_____
_____
_____
_____
_____
_____

Options

How precious also are Your thoughts to me, O God!
How vast is the sum of them! If I should count them, they would
outnumber the sand.
When I awake, I am still with You.

(PSALM 138:17, 18 NASB 1995)

To be or not to be
To walk in darkness and blinded by sin
To choose you Lord as my Savior and king
To focus on the things that I want and don't have
To focus on the many blessings that you give again and again
To complain that I am here
Or to be grateful that I have a place, a home, a shelter from the storm
To complain about the pain I feel when I get up in the morning
Or to thank God that I am not paralyzed and I can feel
To wonder why my sleep is disturbed
Or thank God for meeting me in the early mornings and giving me
words that take me through the day
To focus on the lack of designer clothes and things around me
To complain because I do not have specific names on the clothes that I wear
Instead of focusing on provisions that God has given that fit my need
To focus on others not knowing and understanding me
Instead of relishing in the fact that God knows my name
Knowing that God knows where I am and what I need
Focusing on being chosen by God for certain gifts and talents
Be blessed enough to lay down at night and not fearing danger
Because God has angels all around me watching and protecting
Thanking God for accepting my repentance and calling me His child
and heir

Thanking him for natural vision and glasses to help me see clearer

Thanking Him for spiritual vision to avoid traps that Satan puts in my way

Drowning in sorrow, trouble and despair

Instead of realizing these things come to make me stronger

Not focusing on the darkness in my history

But focusing on how far God had bought me

Thanking God for being transparent and willing to share my testimony of God's deliverance with others

Though I have passed through trouble waters

I choose to thank God that I have not drowned in the waters because he walked with me through them

I have been in valley experiences that took me to the lowest parts of my heart and mind

I choose to thank God because he did not leave me there

Instead, he also gave me mountain experiences and purpose for being on the mountain top

Sometimes he took me places to show me how much he loves me

I choose to trust in a God that shed enough blood to pay for the sin in my life

I choose to trust in my God who makes my little add up become much

I choose to trust my God who subtracts the things in my life that are designed to destroy me

I choose the option where God chooses to divide and remove the things in my life that don't need to be there

I choose God as my option because he keeps multiplying his will in my life

My option is God and God alone

Written as I considered all that God is to and for me on 1/2/2020
© Dr. Cynthia Locke Henderson

God's word is powerful. What does this scripture say to you?

_____

_____

_____

_____

_____

What have you learned during this time with Lord?

_____

_____

_____

_____

_____

Are there things you need to do differently?

_____

_____

_____

_____

_____

Before you leave this moment, write down God's directions to you.

_____

_____

_____

_____

_____

Close this journaling moment with a prayer.

_____

_____

_____

_____

_____

One Ounce Of Faith Is What Fuels My Hope In Christ

He replied, "Because you have so little faith. Truly I tell you, if you have faith as small as a mustard seed, you can say to this mountain, 'Move from here to there,' and it will move. Nothing will be impossible for you."

(MATTHEW 17:20)

Lord, we look around at the conditions and the disorder that this world is in
Man takes life as if he gives it, children are not regarded as our future, unimaginable things occur because of sin
Mass murders destroying life in multiple amounts, drugs illegal then made legal to cover our pain
Bullying among our children and bullying from our government, who do our children have to break this chain

Lord, I have to have faith that my belief in you is not dependent upon what I see in my sight
I must trust in your word that I hear constantly and believe in you God with all my might
You took on the weight of the world, the government is on your shoulder
No matter what it looks like you are always in charge, you are my hope holder and my faith molder

The distraction is to focus on what seems like a larger battle, a destructed force, a monumental task

Believe on your word, walk in your will for me, you hold me accountable to believe in you that is all you ask

I need to focus on sharing your word with all that you direct to cross my path

I must touch one soul, one child, one homeless person, one family, one hopeless one and let you do the math

It is not always in the big things that I feel I must do, Lord you gave yourself freely without complications

You have continued to show yourself proficient, qualified, efficient and competent in every situation

I believe that what I ask in your name and will, will happen

This belief I must live in order to share hope with girls, boys, women and men

"I am the LORD, the God of all mankind. Is anything too hard for me?"
(Jeremiah 32:27)

I am responsible for believing that he makes my impossible, possible!

Written as God instructed me to focus on what I need to do and to avoid the distraction of being overwhelmed © 1/3/2020 Dr. Cynthia Locke Henderson

/ God's word is powerful. What does this scripture say to you?

_____
_____
_____
_____
_____

/ What have you learned during this time with Lord?

_____
_____
_____
_____
_____

/ Are there things you need to do differently?

_____
_____
_____
_____
_____

/ Before you leave this moment, write down God's directions to you.

_____
_____
_____
_____
_____

/ Close this journaling moment with a prayer.

_____
_____
_____
_____
_____

Lord Can I Be
"STRAIGHTFORWARD"
With You

———— ⁓⁓ ————

Dear friends, do not be surprised at the fiery ordeal that has come on you to test you, as though something strange were happening to you.

(1 PETER 4:12)

Lord, pleasing others no matter who they are is becoming obsolete
You meet them and anticipate one outcome only to find out they were not the person you planned to meet
You try with all your heart to start out with integrity, fortitude and a resolve to begin with a clean slate
Gradually and sometime quickly you find out things whose purpose is filled with destruction and hate

Lord, it makes me feel like here I go again, there must be something that I must learn
Lord, I seek to be who you made me, care like you have cared for me, yet before you know it, I feel I have been burned
Lord, I know I am human and these feelings will come repeatedly, please help me have a better after-effect
 Lord, flood me with your word that allows me to know you have not left and that I don't have to be an emotional wreck

Lord, I don't mean to complain, I am glad that I can be straightforward with you because you know what is in my heart
Before I petition or cry out to you, you already know what I am going to ask, even before our conversation starts

My resolve is, I know when I seek you with all my heart and stop my interventions, you will always respond to my need

Help me speak and convey your word, when I serve help me serve with the strength you provide, let me take heed

Lord. what I am gaining in this straightforward mode is that as I draw near to you the space between us shrinks

You increasing become etched in my heart with an indelible mark like permanent ink

No matter where these heart inquiries take me you never allow me to lose courage to press forward with sureness

It may not feel easy when I am in the test, but with confidence, I know I am not alone and your rescue of me is the best

Lord thank you for always giving me you word STRAIGHTFORWARD!

You will seek me and find me when you seek me with all your heart.
Jeremiah 29:13

Written as God instructed me to focus on what I need to do and to avoid the distraction of being overwhelmed© 1/6/2020 Dr. Cynthia Locke Henderson

God's word is powerful. What does this scripture say to you?

_____

_____

_____

_____

_____

What have you learned during this time with Lord?

_____

_____

_____

_____

_____

Are there things you need to do differently?

_____

_____

_____

_____

_____

Before you leave this moment, write down God's directions to you.

_____

_____

_____

_____

_____

Close this journaling moment with a prayer.

_____

_____

_____

_____

_____

_____

Change Your Language

Death and life are in the power of the tongue:
and they that love it shall eat the fruit thereof.

(PROVERBS 18:21)

Lord, as your heir you have given me so much power when I
accepted you as my Lord and Savior
Temptations and trails will come, but nothing more than I am capable of
getting through because you provide a waiver
In those times of temptations and trials you allow me to learn things
that make me strong while in the learning zone
You provide a way of escape when things in the learning zone are more
than I can handle, you never leave me alone

I have to change my language from negativity and not speak death and
destruction to the life granted by thee
Instead of saying what I can't do, you remind me that I can do all things
in your will because you strengthen me
I must not give up and say "I can't" before I even get started, you see that
tongue can be my death
When anxiety comes and makes me think that I am incompetent and
powerless, I have peace in you who gives me wealth

God has given me life, a life to give to myself and to others in what I do
and what I say
It is I that must change my language to reflect God's abundance in all
things that are done according to his way
Somethings will not make me feel happy or somethings may attempt to
destroy God's peace that is within
My language must change, God has prepared me for what comes my
way, I have all that I need to obtain Christ's win

The "I can't" that emanates from my tongue should be, "I can't go wrong" with the power that Christ gives!

And God is able to bless you abundantly, so that in all things at all times, having all that you need, you will abound in every good work. (2 Corinthians 9:8)

Writing during my morning talk with God as he reminds me that the source of my needs, wants and desire are his to grant.© 1/7/2020 Dr. Cynthia Locke Henderson

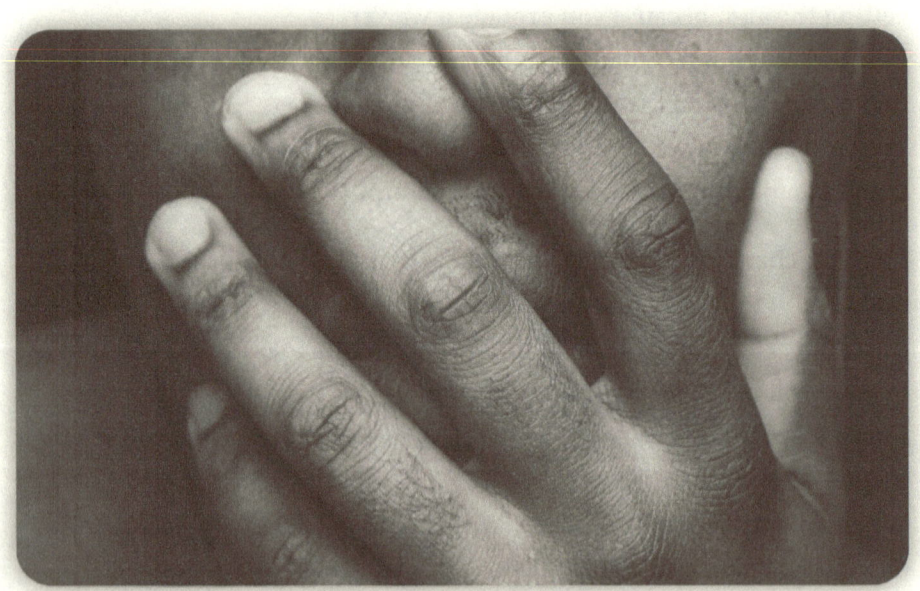

_ God's word is powerful. What does this scripture say to you?

_____

_____

_____

_____

_____

_ What have you learned during this time with Lord?

_____

_____

_____

_____

_____

_ Are there things you need to do differently?

_____

_____

_____

_____

_____

_ Before you leave this moment, write down God's directions to you.

_____

_____

_____

_____

_____

_ Close this journaling moment with a prayer.

_____

_____

_____

_____

_____

_____

Abide

If you abide in Me, and My words abide in you, you will ask what you
desire, and it shall be done for you.

(JOHN 15:7 NKJV)

Lord, in order to abide in you, it takes all of me to fully abide
When I am in my secret place where no one knows how many times in
this place I have cried
I must abide in you in those moments because you care about the things
that I can only bring to you
My viewpoint must be, that there is no substitute for remedying the
things I ask for you to do

Thou I seek others to fix my issue, thou I trust in tangible things that I
posses
My answers come when I give all to you, confess to you and give room
for you to bless
Abiding in you does not mean praying to you but seeking a solution that
has no power like you
You promise me that if I come to you, you will give rest, before I ask for
help, my needs you already knew

Abiding in you does not mean I trade off to get things that are not in
your will
Abiding in you is not doing it my way when you have already promised
to fight my battles if I be still
Abiding does not mean giving my difficulties, my struggles to you and
taking them back
Abiding is trusting you when the enemy attacks, trusting you to always
help me stay on track

Lord help me ABIDE 100%

Come close to God, and God will come close to you.

Wash your hands, you sinners; purify your hearts, for your loyalty is divided between God and the world.
(James 4:8 NLT)

Written as I came empty to God this morning needing him to give me directions ©
1/7/2020 Dr. Cynthia Locke Henderson

God's word is powerful. What does this scripture say to you?

_____

_____

_____

_____

_____

What have you learned during this time with Lord?

_____

_____

_____

_____

_____

Are there things you need to do differently?

_____

_____

_____

_____

_____

Before you leave this moment, write down God's directions to you.

_____

_____

_____

_____

_____

Close this journaling moment with a prayer.

_____

_____

_____

_____

_____

In Between Time

He will cover you with his feathers. He will shelter you with his wings.
His faithful promises are your armor and protection. Do not be afraid
of the terrors of the night, nor the arrow that flies in the day.

(PSALM 91:4-5 NLT)

Today I am in between what I have been through and where I am
going next
I am in between the messages you give in the Bible your holy text
The words seem to bring a different but similar message no matter if I
read the same verse on a different day
Your word gives strength that at some point in this in between space I
am able to say come what may

Lord, I am learning to trust you because you are my keeper and sustainer
Trusting in you is only a receipt for all the things that you have developed, in my in between space, you are my trainer
Lord, natural circumstance could have taken from me, but you keep me
connected for the plans you have for me
Though the plans seem unachievable, bigger than me, unreachable, you
always kept me moving forward to thee

Lord, that space in between my time has been uniquely customized to
sculpture me into your hidden figure
Man has tried to make me into his sculpture by things they say and do,
but none can match your design configure
Lord, I yield to you - my joy, my peace, my keeper, my friend, my maker
my strength in between time
I will not share myself and I know you will help me to never share me
with another sculptor while on your assembly line

Lord, please stay with me in between time

If you make the LORD your refuge, if you make the Most High, your shelter, no evil will conquer you; no plague will come near your home. (Psalm 91:9-10 NLT)

Inspired by my amazing God on 1/9/2020 Dr. Cynthia Locke Henderson

God's word is powerful. What does this scripture say to you?

_____
_____
_____
_____
_____

What have you learned during this time with Lord?

_____
_____
_____
_____
_____

Are there things you need to do differently?

_____
_____
_____
_____
_____

Before you leave this moment, write down God's directions to you.

_____
_____
_____
_____
_____

Close this journaling moment with a prayer.

_____
_____
_____
_____
_____
_____

Invisible Blessings

———— ✤ ————

Who among the gods is like you, LORD? Who is like you—majestic in holiness, awesome in glory, working wonders?

(Exodus 15:11)

Lord, you placed so many blessings in my existence
Over time as I had needs and wants you have always been consistent
There were times when I felt I did not have enough of things
Still you knew what was best so some things you did not choose to bring

Some things that I wanted in my life I was not prepared to receive
Some things I wanted I did not whole heartedly believe
You gave me time to grow and understand what you had for me and
what I could not handle
If you gave everything that I felt I wanted my life would be a living scandal

So, you blessed me to love in the midst of painful scars and emptiness
You blessed me with the love of my children, the love of giving love and
the love of having less
Lord you blessed me to think, to remember and be content with your
management
I am blessed today because you keep goodness and mercy surrounding
me while you are always present

I am genuinely blessed with things that can't be measured or contained
in a box, I am blessed with God
I can cry because of pain that can't be seen only to cry later at the miraculous power of God's directing rod
I can be in the mist of chaos only to feel it dissipate as God moves the
confusion and brings peace
There is none like you God who decreases when needed and removes
lack and replace it with increase

Written as inspired by God during our time together on 1/9/2020 Dr. Cynthia L. Henderson

God's word is powerful. What does this scripture say to you?

_____
_____
_____
_____
_____

What have you learned during this time with Lord?

_____
_____
_____
_____
_____

Are there things you need to do differently?

_____
_____
_____
_____
_____

Before you leave this moment, write down God's directions to you.

_____
_____
_____
_____
_____

Close this journaling moment with a prayer.

_____
_____
_____
_____
_____
_____

Lord You Can Read Me Inside And Out

See if there is any offensive way in me, and lead me
in the way everlasting.

(PSALM 139:24)

Lord, I am like a book with the perfect cover and
an intriguing invitation to read it
But you oh Lord, know what is within my book and that everything in
me does not acknowledge the spirit
I pray this day, the way that you search within me, for those things you
do not approve for my heart
Help me to acknowledge them when you expose their pages and set
them apart

Help me understand the damage that those pages had done and the
continued damage that they can bring
Lord, it is painful when you reveal the things that should not be there,
help me let go down to the final string
There is no need to hide those pages that should not be in my heart
because you see and know the location
You have plans for me but the offensive things within my book cannot
be your selective foundation

I come to you because too much time has been wasted and hidden
behind the cover of my story
I yield to your will, repenting and trusting you to use my life to get the
glory

The cover of my book of me must match inside and out
if I am to walk in your everlasting way
Simply put, Lord rewrite my story, remove the offensive way, help me
obtain a pure heart, one that will not sway

Read me Lord Inside and out.

Written I began my 21 days of dangerous prayer 1/12/2020
© Dr. Cynthia Locke Henderson

🖊 God's word is powerful. What does this scripture say to you?

_____

_____

_____

_____

_____

🖊 What have you learned during this time with Lord?

_____

_____

_____

_____

_____

🖊 Are there things you need to do differently?

_____

_____

_____

_____

_____

🖊 Before you leave this moment, write down God's directions to you.

_____

_____

_____

_____

_____

🖊 Close this journaling moment with a prayer.

_____

_____

_____

_____

_____

My Heart Needs Intervention From You

Even though I walk through the darkest valley, I will fear no evil, for you are with me; your rod and your staff, they comfort me.

(PSALM 23:4)

Lord, when I stop and take inventory of my life thus far
There have been battles after battles followed by moments that cause reflect on my heart scare
It seems to come back to the same areas, how much of this can I take
I have smiles and happy moments but then I have aches

I ask you for keeping power that tells me you are who I must love whole heartedly first
I think I hurt sometimes when I don't have to, your love must be enough even in the worst
Lord I have lost too much time conceding to pain that takes me off of my path
Thank you for not giving up and always being there in the aftermath

Lord I seek to love you so much that consistency of trust is my weapon in combat
I seek your intervention so that I keep the breastplate of righteousness when under attack

Thank you for shortening my moments of retreat, with you word and with your instruction
Thank you for saving me from destruction and molding me like you under your construction

Lord you are my sustainer, my maintainer, my retainer, my container, you are my riches asset!!!

Written during my dangerous prayer on 1/13/2020 © Dr. Cynthia Locke Henderson

God's word is powerful. What does this scripture say to you?

_____
_____
_____
_____
_____

What have you learned during this time with Lord?

_____
_____
_____
_____
_____

Are there things you need to do differently?

_____
_____
_____
_____
_____

Before you leave this moment, write down God's directions to you.

_____
_____
_____
_____
_____

Close this journaling moment with a prayer.

_____
_____
_____
_____
_____

You Chose Me

Lord, you chose me, how blessed I am, how great to know I was your selection
A lot went into making me come to this point in my life, I am understanding that more in my reflection
You chose my mom, a woman that frequently warned me that you would not make me endure things I could not bearYou knew my father would not be there so you allowed her to love me enough without a father's care

It seemed that I always had to go the extra mile and seemed to have a bountiful share of things to occur
There were moments that you allowed me to shine, then so many things to happen that was not what I prefer
But through it all I learned to trust you, take risks without fear, walk many times alone, and cry out for you often
As I learned to say thy kingdom come, thy will be done, and dared to trust you, my anxiousness was softened

Lord. I am growing up and still have lots of room for learning and growth
I am learning to give my life more to your purpose and to take this oath
To love you the way you teach me and the desire to fulfill YOUR purpose not mine
There are factors and people that you allow linkage and movement to your purpose, thank you for the ties that bind

Lord forgive my debts as I forgive my debtors, they do not owe me, when you are in charge of all that happens for me.

Give us today our daily bread. And forgive us our debts, as we also have forgiven our debtors. (Matthews 6:11-12)

🖊 God's word is powerful. What does this scripture say to you?

_____

_____

_____

_____

_____

🖊 What have you learned during this time with Lord?

_____

_____

_____

_____

_____

🖊 Are there things you need to do differently?

_____

_____

_____

_____

_____

🖊 Before you leave this moment, write down God's directions to you.

_____

_____

_____

_____

_____

🖊 Close this journaling moment with a prayer.

_____

_____

_____

_____

_____

Reveal Me To Me

See, I have engraved you on the palms of my hands;
your walls are ever before me.

(ISAIAH 49:16)

Lord, just when I think I know who I am and how I will respond to a situation and a circumstance
Something and someone come along and causes me to pause wondering if I can maintain my stance
Deep in side of my heart I know you are revealing a part me to me for improvement and growth
Lord I make all kinds of excuses saying that what I am experiencing is not the real me, that I loath

At this time, this place that I have arrived in my life, I yield to asking you to examine and reveal me to me
Those things that don't belong in you plans for me, please help me to let go so that I am free
I may not always feel that I am getting a fair share in what you show me and what you reveal
Lord help me know exactly what I need to know about me so that I began to heal

Lord you are my coach in this game of finding my way and place in your will
Please let me not be distracted by people, their deception and what I feel
Feeling is one thing, but knowing that I belong to you and that I am truly your heir
Gives me assurance that no matter what, Lord no matter where you are always there

Lord I hold on to you and have confidence that you know me and you know my name, there is no substitution for that!

Be strong and courageous. Do not be afraid or terrified because of them, for the LORD your God goes with you; he will never leave you nor forsake you." (Deuteronomy 31:6)

Written as you inspired me, comforted me and coaches me through life 1/15/2020 © Dr. Cynthia Locke Henderson

God's word is powerful. What does this scripture say to you?

_____
_____
_____
_____
_____

What have you learned during this time with Lord?

_____
_____
_____
_____
_____

Are there things you need to do differently?

_____
_____
_____
_____
_____

Before you leave this moment, write down God's directions to you.

_____
_____
_____
_____
_____

Close this journaling moment with a prayer.

_____
_____
_____
_____
_____

Lord I Need "Leveling Out"

He heals the brokenhearted and binds up their wounds.

(PSALM 147:3)

Lord, enough is enough, sometimes up and sometimes down, sometime happy sometimes not
Sometimes I walk with a determination to withstand the inconsistent leveling instead of resting on what you taught
Lord, it seems some big things come and shake my balance and some little things come and shake my faith
Lord there are days that I want to run for you through every test, trial, distractor but something interrupts my pace

Lord, you already know that I am unlevel and I need consistent obedience to respond to your guidance
You continue to plant your words and works into me that reminds me that I need compliance
I am not going to always be perfect, but I have an ear let me hear with heart, let me see with my soul
Lord, I know I need leveling out, teach me how to level my spirit so that I can close every single hole

Lord, I believe that only you can level me out, and that is why it is for you that I cry out
Lord, help rest on the fact, you are the God that heals me, heals the wounds and removes the doubt
Disruptions in my path will cause struggles, you always deliver, it's not all about me, so I share my story
So other see that you will level us out of struggles, disruptions so that we get victory and you get GLORY

Lord, I understand that life is a process that matters with my obedience and your guidance!

"'Nevertheless, I will bring health and healing to it; I will heal my people and will let them enjoy abundant peace and security."
(Jeremiah 33:6)

Inspired by God and the hope that I have in his orchestrating of my life.
1/16/2020 © Dr. Cynthia Locke Henderson

Balance that can't be defined by man

God's word is powerful. What does this scripture say to you?

_____

_____

_____

_____

_____

What have you learned during this time with Lord?

_____

_____

_____

_____

_____

Are there things you need to do differently?

_____

_____

_____

_____

_____

Before you leave this moment, write down God's directions to you.

_____

_____

_____

_____

_____

Close this journaling moment with a prayer.

_____

_____

_____

_____

_____

Lord I Am Sorry For Ignoring Your Presence

Lord for all of the years of my life, you have been in the space I call my space
You have placed angles that I have simply not acknowledged and would not embrace
It is not an accident that you wake me every morning and you shut this body down when it needs rest
There have been so many days that are filled with ambivalence, restlessness, aloneness and excessive stress

How could I miss your presence, you preserved my heart from taking on much more than it could handle
When aloneness is in my space, you protect and keep fear from dominating my thoughts, you keep me from the vandal
It is not my own ability that tells me to go a different way today, or slows my trip to help avoid danger that lies ahead
Often, I am reminded that if I had not listened, and detoured to accomplish my desire, that I could have been dead

Lord I am so sorry for every time that I ignored your presence, yet you saved me and protected me from harm
Right now, I recognize your presence as I cry out for more of you, I am aware that you recognize me in your arms
When I hear about so many dangerous and deadly events far away and some close to my space
I am sorry that I have not acknowledged that you had angels around me face to face

There are bullets that had my name on them, but you dared them to touch me because I am yours

There are many times I say, that car just missed me or times I have been in the midst of dangers, I can't keep the scores

There have been times that my pockets were empty and I did not know where my resources would originate,

With nothing in the bank, no one coming to my rescue, you stepped in a situation that could have been my fate

Do not be afraid of the terrors of the night, nor the arrow that flies in the day.

He will cover you with his feathers. He will shelter you with his wings. His faithful promises are your armor and protection. Do not be afraid of the terrors of the night, nor the arrow that flies in the day.
(Psalm 91:4, 5 NLT)

Written as God reminded me that his angels are in my presence 24/7 on assignment by Him. Oh my God Thank You 1/17/2020 © Dr. Cynthia Locke Henderson

God's word is powerful. What does this scripture say to you?

_____

_____

_____

_____

_____

What have you learned during this time with Lord?

_____

_____

_____

_____

_____

Are there things you need to do differently?

_____

_____

_____

_____

_____

Before you leave this moment, write down God's directions to you.

_____

_____

_____

_____

_____

Close this journaling moment with a prayer.

_____

_____

_____

_____

_____

_____

The Plot

"Come to me, all you who are weary and burdened,
and I will give you rest.

(Matthew 11:28)

Lord, it seems we have moments of peace and rest in you when
things so quickly turn upside down
Our smile and contentment in you are replaced by a heaviness in our
soul and an overwhelming breakdown
Our feelings are taken off of you and replaced by feelings that we can
handle this attack again us
We trust in our astuteness and skillfulness, rather than, in God putting
all of or trust

Lord, please help us return to your trust and promise, that you never
abandon in the midst of plots crafted to destroy
Plots to take us off our paths to destiny, plots to overpower, plots to
cause devastation and plots to steal joy
Please help me pull from the strength that you give in your word, the
companionship of the Holy Spirit's protection
You know the plots that are crafted against me as I try to do your will,
help me retreat to your divine fortification

How quickly I seem to forget that you care and do not leave me on the
battlefield alone looking for a place to run
I am one of yours, among millions, billions, trillions yet you uniquely
preserve as if I am your only one
Lest I never forget your promise to care always, you promise to get me
through every plot to destroy my destiny
No matter what scheme are organized against me, you know my name,
you know what I am made of, you got me

Lord it is mandatory that I never forget you power of mercy, grace, restoration and strength! Like Job, danger can come near me but it cannot destroy my soul. That is why I MUST cry out to you Lord

What then shall we say in response to these things? If God is for us, who can be against us? Romans 8:31

Written as God reminded me that "He has got me".
1/182020 © Dr. Cynthia Locke Henderson

🖊 God's word is powerful. What does this scripture say to you?

_____

_____

_____

_____

_____

🖊 What have you learned during this time with Lord?

_____

_____

_____

_____

_____

🖊 Are there things you need to do differently?

_____

_____

_____

_____

_____

🖊 Before you leave this moment, write down God's directions to you.

_____

_____

_____

_____

_____

🖊 Close this journaling moment with a prayer.

_____

_____

_____

_____

_____

Lord I Need An Answer

Hear my prayer, LORD; listen to my cry for mercy.
When I am in distress, I call to you, because you answer me.

(PSALM 86: 6, 7)

Going a little farther, he fell with his face to the ground and prayed,
"My Father, if it is possible, may this cup be taken from me. Yet not as
I will, but as you will."

(MATTHEW 26:39)

Lord, daily I am learning that I simply do not want to continue with whining and moving without direction
My understanding of unfairness, my feelings of "I have had enough" are not the right choice and selection
There are times when you want us to stand in firmness and there are times when you want us silent
When we whine and move without your help, we surrender to emotional violence

Responding to what feels like a repeated period or a long time being disregarded may not be on your timing
There can be additional things that I need to learn, I am sure you have a plan, perhaps I am not finished climbing
Lord you elevate us according to what you see in us and the purpose that you have for us as you raise us up
But Lord I feel like I have had enough of this circumstance, take it away, I don't to drink from this cup

Lord as I look to you for my answer, I humbly understand that it is not my will, Lord thy will be my conclusion
Please release me from complaining and fortify my strength and help me remove all my confusion

Lord you give me help in this troubling time, help me to know that help from man is useless

Lord you are my solution, you are my keeper, you have all the answers I need your presence to pass this test

Thank you for answering me and helping me listen. I must keep my eyes on the prize.

Give us help from trouble, for the help of man is useless.
(Psalm 60:11 NKJV)

Written as God had a heart-to-heart talk with me, and answered me quickly.
On 1/21/20 © Dr. Cynthia Locke Henderson

🖊 God's word is powerful. What does this scripture say to you?

_____
_____
_____
_____
_____

🖊 What have you learned during this time with Lord?

_____
_____
_____
_____
_____

🖊 Are there things you need to do differently?

_____
_____
_____
_____
_____

🖊 Before you leave this moment, write down God's directions to you.

_____
_____
_____
_____
_____

🖊 Close this journaling moment with a prayer.

_____
_____
_____
_____
_____

There Was A Second Set Of Footprints Next To Mine In The Footprints Of Time

———— ⁕⳥⳽⳿ ————

Cease striving and know that I am God; I will be exalted among the nations; I will be exalted in the earth.

(PSALM 46:10 NASB 1995)

Lord, my life is not worth anything if I have not used it to show the world that you are King over all

What I do in life connects to what you do in and through me no matter how big or how small

My feet have gone many places that I would never have had an opportunity or power to get me there

Often, I have wondered, how did my mange to arrive in places of importance, it was not my power it was my prayer

Greater than my prayers were the need to have you answer those prayers and allowing me to leave an imprint

For every footprint I leave, has another divine footprint next to mine indicating you walked with me and left your print

God author the legacies in my life, I pray that others come to know that only you sent opportunities my way

There are so many things that have occurred in my life because of the way you created my heart to function day by day

Lord, please help me know with assurance that all this time my foot prints in the sands of time were ordered by you

Lord, thank you for allowing me to leave something that bless others or shows that you are in charge of what I do

There is no way that I could imagine how I do the things I do, help me avoid responding to strife

Make my motive pure; help me to do and give your way, your rewards leave legacies of you in my life

Lord I in awe of what you do in my life, all that you have deposited in me. You give me purpose for the day.

And we know that in all things God works for the good of those who love him, who have been called according to his purpose. Romans 8:28

in all your ways submit to him, and he will make your paths straight. (Proverbs 3:6)

Written as God made me aware that he is building a legacy in me worth leaving for the world on 1/22/20 20 © Dr. Cynthia Locke Henderson

God's word is powerful. What does this scripture say to you?

_____
_____
_____
_____
_____

What have you learned during this time with Lord?

_____
_____
_____
_____
_____

Are there things you need to do differently?

_____
_____
_____
_____
_____

Before you leave this moment, write down God's directions to you.

_____
_____
_____
_____
_____

Close this journaling moment with a prayer.

_____
_____
_____
_____
_____

Thanks For Bringing Light To My Dark Places

Let the peace of Christ rule in your hearts, since as members of one body you were called to peace. And be thankful.

(COLOSSIANS 3:15)

Lord, thank you for exposing my dark places to me
Thank you for not allowing me to be comfortable there and helping find the light within thee
Lord, there was more anger in that place than I need to have, along with that anger was pain
Along with the pain where chains holding down my victory and causing a thunderous rain

Lord, you came in there, you did not let me be alone, you carefully removed the darkness and stain
Lord as I praised you the darkness began to leave as I felt your strength breaking the chain
You move anger, hurt, frustration, disappointment until your peace inside of me sent darkness down the drain
Lord in those moments I learned to acknowledge the darkness release it and allow your peace to be the main

Lord thank you for removing the darkness that was taking me out of my lane
The clouds of darkness were replaced with forgiveness and made my sight of you love very plane
Lord I am tired of this roller coaster ride making me feel like a wrecked unsteady train

What a ride it was before I could see that all I needed to do was give it to you and remove the blame

Pain, stain, rain, blame, insane, untamed
before I found my way back to my lane!

And the peace of God, which transcends all understanding, will guard your hearts and your minds in Christ Jesus. (Philippians 4:7)

When the LORD takes pleasure in anyone's way, he causes their enemies to make peace with them. (Proverbs 16:7)

Written in recovery of a dark place while God talked to me.
1/23/2020 © Dr. Cynthia Locke Henderson

I Am Your Diamond, Lord

God's word is powerful. What does this scripture say to you?

_____
_____
_____
_____
_____

What have you learned during this time with Lord?

_____
_____
_____
_____
_____

Are there things you need to do differently?

_____
_____
_____
_____
_____

Before you leave this moment, write down God's directions to you.

_____
_____
_____
_____
_____

Close this journaling moment with a prayer.

_____
_____
_____
_____
_____

Time Does Not Belong To Me

Lord, I have learned that my expectations should not be in how I think life should be nor in what I call maturity

People's commitments are constantly changing, rearranging my life, they do not possess my security

First, I must repent for wasting time and trying to measure it against my standards and expectation

My time belongs to God and every second I waste weaken my hope and alertness to what God has for my foundation

When my time is used according to the purpose God has for me, all things fit like a puzzle and work together

No matter what come my way, no matter what seems to be taken away, no matter the shifts in the weather

I know that God will weather whatever storms come in my life, for he is in control of the storm

Storms come robust and strong giving feelings of fear, doubt, failure causing us to lose time as they form

So, I turn my expectation and hope on God and what he has crafted for my time on this earth

I know he has a plan for me to prosper and be in good health, a plan he has had since my birth

In my eyes a lot of time has passed and what lies ahead seems limited, short, and far ahead

The Lord has crafted the fibers of my life, input his design and purpose, together he is stitching every single thread

My hope is the finish product as I remain available for his design.

From one man he made all the nations, that they should inhabit the whole earth; and he marked out their appointed times in history and the boundaries of their lands. (Act 17:26)

Written as God gave me a lesson about time on 1/23/2020 © Dr. Cynthia L. Henderson

God's word is powerful. What does this scripture say to you?

_____
_____
_____
_____
_____

What have you learned during this time with Lord?

_____
_____
_____
_____
_____

Are there things you need to do differently?

_____
_____
_____
_____
_____

Before you leave this moment, write down God's directions to you.

_____
_____
_____
_____
_____

Close this journaling moment with a prayer.

_____
_____
_____
_____
_____
_____

I Need Heart Surgery

Our human hearts manage the flow of blood to all of our major organs to fuel life and our existence
As it flushed out metabolic waste and waste produce that keeps us from going the distance with resistance
Our sinful souls receive salvation because of the blood that Jesus shed on calvary many years ago, yet it is still strong
We challenge the blood of Jesus when we go contrary to its purpose to right all things in our life gone wrong

My spiritual heart connects my attitude, my desires, my obedience, my willingness and God's spiritual regulation
My heart is in disrepair when I am not able to forgive, when dominated by brokenness and frustration
My heart is in disrepair when I ignore you and do things my way, when I turn my back on your direction
Lord, my spiritual heart is clogged by unnecessary waste, your righteousness does not flow and need correction

Lord, I will trust in you as my surgeon, I trust your tool of forgiveness and the implant of worship and praise
I commit to replacing the dry places in my life with a thirst for you when I feel heartbroken and, in a daze,
Lord, I trust you to mend my ways, cleanse my sins, change my motives, implant your compass for direction
I trust you to put my heart together in such a way that I feel your presences and never lose your connection

Lord take me, fix my heart, so that I am available to you

Written during my consultation with God; my surgeon; 1/25/20 © Dr. Cynthia L. Henderson

God's word is powerful. What does this scripture say to you?

_____
_____
_____
_____
_____

What have you learned during this time with Lord?

_____
_____
_____
_____
_____

Are there things you need to do differently?

_____
_____
_____
_____
_____

Before you leave this moment, write down God's directions to you.

_____
_____
_____
_____
_____

Close this journaling moment with a prayer.

_____
_____
_____
_____
_____
_____

I Am Living Because Of Mercy

———— ⚘ ————

With all my heart I praise the LORD, and with all that I am
I praise his holy name! With all my heart I praise the LORD!
I will never forget how kind he has been. The LORD forgives
our sins, heals us when we are sick, and protects us from death.
His kindness and love are a crown on our heads.

(PSALM 103:1-4 CEV)

Lord, I was born on your mercy, there was nothing that I did to invite me into existence

Despite all circumstantial happening; a child giving birth to child, my birth was because of your insistence

You had the people in place to make sure that I arrived on the time you destined to be

That day that I would honor for every year, and come to realized it was because of thee

Lord, what have I done with the mercy that implied you showed me unmerited favor

Over and over when I have stepped out of your will, the blood of your son has provided me a waiver

Lord illness, near accidents and actual accidents, harm by others, sufferings, and sin

You know all the wrong things that I have done, things I have said and the places I have been

This moment, I repent to you for sin and thank you for keeping mercy around me because of my imperfection

My day begins with new mercies, only you know how it will end, only you keep my mercy connection

Lord today, help me treat each moment like the gift it is and live it like you have directed in your word

No matter where, Lord you are worthy of my praise no matter what, let my THANK YOU be heard

THANK YOU THANK YOU THANK YOU THANK YOU
THANK YOU

Praise the LORD because he is good to us, and his love never fails.
(I Chronicles 16:34 CEV)

Written during my consultation with God; my surgeon;
1/27/2020 © Dr. Cynthia Locke Henderson

God's word is powerful. What does this scripture say to you?

_____

_____

_____

_____

_____

What have you learned during this time with Lord?

_____

_____

_____

_____

_____

Are there things you need to do differently?

_____

_____

_____

_____

_____

Before you leave this moment, write down God's directions to you.

_____

_____

_____

_____

_____

Close this journaling moment with a prayer.

_____

_____

_____

_____

_____

I Am Confident That You Are Molding Me

Yet you, LORD, are our Father. We are the clay, you are the potter; we are all the work of your hand.

(ISAIAH 64:8)

Lord, you have been working hard to perfect me into something and someone useful

You are shaping from the outside and making sure my core is designed to be fruitful

You see and know all the places that have cracks and holds that need repair

Being the caring sculpture that you are you give intervention to the crack and holes with loving care

I know that I am a piece of work that requires your sustaining touch to create clay that is intrafusal

It detects when the amount and rate in the shifting of the clay until it meets your approval

You are molding me in such a way that you know where to put extra spackling to withstand the pressure

You and only you know when the pressure is overwhelming and when I am in need of a refresher

My God, how awesome you are, how skillful you are, how specific you are with my design

I yield to your handy work, I yield to your exposure of my flaws and keeping me in line

It does not always feel good and the molding seems very, very long

However long, I know that in the day of completion to you and only you do I belong

Lord, I don't belong to myself; I belong to you.

*"Call to me, and I will answer you; I will tell you wonderful and marvelous things that you know nothing about.
(Jeremiah 33:3 GNT)*

Written during my consultation with God; my surgeon;
1/28/2020 © Dr. Cynthia Locke Henderson

God's word is powerful. What does this scripture say to you?

_____
_____
_____
_____
_____

What have you learned during this time with Lord?

_____
_____
_____
_____
_____

Are there things you need to do differently?

_____
_____
_____
_____
_____

Before you leave this moment, write down God's directions to you.

_____
_____
_____
_____
_____

Close this journaling moment with a prayer.

_____
_____
_____
_____
_____

Wait On The Lord

Yet the LORD longs to be gracious to you; therefore,
he will rise up to show you compassion. For the LORD is
a God of justice. Blessed are all who wait for him!

(ISAIAH 30:18)

We started out our Christian journey at the peak of our energy
We wanted to do nothing but breathe God when we talk, breathe God
when we walk, we had his synergy
Our will was to do only what he wanted and do it his way
We focused on pleasing him in life every single day

We were on a mission to save the world, bring everyone we touch to
received salvation
It seemed we allowed God to control everything we did to show his
manifestation
We prayed for everything, every move, and wanted nothing that did not
include him
We only went were we felt God had a presence, we wanted to remain in
his realm

Then life happened and we began to transition our thought to our self
It seemed that we lessen our focus on God and places him on a shelf
He did not take his focus off of us, he watched us still
He was our father and his love for us is real

We have experienced life and finally landed in a space where we noticed
that God remained the whole time
He never left us, he just allowed us to learn by experience that he was
not temporary, but fulltime

It seems we wasted so much time swimming in despair, hurting from self-inflicted distress and wrong
Now God who never left us is joyous to have his prodigal heirs to return home

Lord I am ready to do things your way!

Written as God came to my rescue on, 1/29/2020 © Dr. Cynthia Locke Henderson

God's word is powerful. What does this scripture say to you?

_____
_____
_____
_____
_____

What have you learned during this time with Lord?

_____
_____
_____
_____
_____

Are there things you need to do differently?

_____
_____
_____
_____
_____

Before you leave this moment, write down God's directions to you.

_____
_____
_____
_____
_____

Close this journaling moment with a prayer.

_____
_____
_____
_____
_____

A Bag Of Wants
Can Cause Devastation

LORD, you are my God; I will exalt you and praise your name,
for in perfect faithfulness you have done wonderful things,
things planned long ago.

(ISAIAH 25:1)

Lord, I have been on this earth for a while, living because you determined that I should be here
I was born wanting things, milk when hungry, change of diet as I grew, yet my wants did not disappear
As I grew the line between my wants, my desire and my need seem to collide
When things did not favor my wants as a child and as an adult, I cried

As I grew to understand that I needed to understand your faithfulness to me was compared to a bird
You reminded me that a bird does not sow, neither. do they reap, nor gather into barns, they exist undeterred
Yet as I reminisce you provided my wants and never left me in a state of need
Just when life seem to take a turn and I was without what I thought I needed you provided at a "right now" speed

Lord, you have been faithful over the years, your teaching has been perfect when I trust what you say
My bag of wants is decreasing as I have figured out that you set my agenda, you know what I need day after day
You know when I need safety, when I need direction, when I simply need to know how much I matter

You have planned me, my life, my experiences, my need for balance giving me the desire to let my wants scatter

You are my father and never give up you position in my life. I thank you Lord

Whom have I in heaven but You? And besides You, I desire nothing on earth. My flesh and my heart may fail, But God is the strength of my heart and my portion forever.
(Psalm 73:25,26 NASB 1995)

Written as God came to my rescue on, 1/30/2020 © Dr. Cynthia Locke Henderson

God's word is powerful. What does this scripture say to you?

_____

_____

_____

_____

_____

What have you learned during this time with Lord?

_____

_____

_____

_____

_____

Are there things you need to do differently?

_____

_____

_____

_____

_____

Before you leave this moment, write down God's directions to you.

_____

_____

_____

_____

_____

Close this journaling moment with a prayer.

_____

_____

_____

_____

_____

You Waited

Because you are with me, I will not fear trepidations, I will hold on.

Lord, no matter my situation, whether it was for me to learn something I needed to know,
You waited because that was the way I needed to learn, and the way to help me grow
I made more mistakes in life than I can ever count
Knowing that you still waited, for my trust in you was paramount

Some of things that I went through, I had to repeat because I missed the lesson, you were trying to teach
Yet through it all, Lord waited patiently until I shared with others you wanted to reach
I am learning, daily that nothing in my life happens by chance
You waited until my lessons were completed, and my ways were saturated with a Godly enhance

Lord, you waited until I reached this year, this month, this week, this day, this moment, this second
You waited to make sure I knew what it meant to have faith, and to make sure I responded when you beckoned
You waited to give strength, you waited to give healing, you waited until I really came acquainted with the great, I AM
You waited for me to I know your love was not a scam, you waited until I connected completely to Jesus, the LAMB

Lord, whatever my lot in life, it is well with my soul because, YOU WAITED FOR ME.

When you pass through the waters, I will be with you; and when you pass through the rivers, they will not sweep over you. When you walk through the fire, you will not be burned; the flames will not set you ablaze. (Isaiah 43:2)

Written as God came to my rescue on, 1/31/2020 © Dr. Cynthia Locke Henderson

God's word is powerful. What does this scripture say to you?

_____

_____

_____

_____

_____

What have you learned during this time with Lord?

_____

_____

_____

_____

_____

Are there things you need to do differently?

_____

_____

_____

_____

_____

Before you leave this moment, write down God's directions to you.

_____

_____

_____

_____

_____

Close this journaling moment with a prayer.

_____

_____

_____

_____

_____

My Level Of Trust Is Equal To My Response To God

———— ⚬⚬ ————

Lord, when I say use me or I am available to you do - my actions show that I mean it
Am I really ready to make the necessary shifts in my thoughts, my obedience and something just simply quit?
Am I ready to stop the questions: "Why me? Why do I have to do it this way? Why do I have to do it today?"
Lord, I find myself telling God that I think it would be better if I did it differently from what you say

My level of trust = My response to God

Lord, please help me to trust that you will move mountains or give me what I need to climb them
When I am surrounded by evil, hatred, jealousy and malice, help me transfer my thoughts to your heavenly realm
Lord, too often I think I am not good enough, help me trust you and walk places that I could never visualize
When you place me in places and open the door for me to speak, give me word to say and verbalize

My level of trust = My response to God

Lord, life is so full of human elements that have limited authority and has inadequate control
Lord with faith small as a mustard seed, I trust that you will reward my obedience to know that you protect my soul
Lord, it is my heart's desire to increase the math for my level of trust, to

be directly control how I respond to you

This day I commit to trusting you with decisions, where I go, when to respond, and letting mistrust become few

Trust in the LORD with all your heart and lean not on your own understanding. (Proverbs 3:5)

Written as God came to my rescue on, 2/1/2020 © Dr. Cynthia Locke Henderson

God's word is powerful. What does this scripture say to you?

_____

_____

_____

_____

_____

What have you learned during this time with Lord?

_____

_____

_____

_____

_____

Are there things you need to do differently?

_____

_____

_____

_____

_____

Before you leave this moment, write down God's directions to you.

_____

_____

_____

_____

_____

Close this journaling moment with a prayer.

_____

_____

_____

_____

_____

PUSH

But a time is coming, and it is already here! Even now the true
worshipers are being led by the Spirit to worship the Father according
to the truth. These are the ones the Father is seeking to worship him.

(JOHN 4:23 CEV)

Lord, you have opened our hearts to expose what is not there and
identified what should be there

In our house, or soul, were things we knew were there and thing hid that
we did not want to share

We realized that daily we had a lot of learning to do, but required you to
teach us to do things your way

We were willing and available to move to a place where you could fulfil
your purpose day by day

Then Lord you began to test and examine our genuineness and authenticity to see if our desire was from our heart

We yielded our imperfection, our vulnerability and asked for restoration
and another chance to start

We had to PUSH

Lord, the hunger down in us was not for food, we desperately prayed for
you removed all that offends you

Lord then you answered us as a father would to his crying child and told
us to stop whining and do what you say do

Lord, we realized that we were leaving a legacy that was not worthy of all
that you do for us

We asked for a change in our legacy to out shine anything in our hearts
but to show in you we trust

Lord, out of exhaustion from whining, and realizing you never left us
and that you wanted us willingly

We want your face to shine on us as we surrendered freely and

announced our availability

We had to PUSH

Acknowledging that too many things had been done our way and not according to you plan

We asked for forgiveness and mercy as we now see that we can fall for anything but for you we must stand

We had to take our hands off the potter wheel and realize that you are the sculptor of us all

You are the one that straighten the wrinkles, fill the holes, you Lord, are the one who molds us it's your call

Opposition will come and it will come hard, help how I respond, so please help us finish this process in line

Please help us move forward with truthful lips, a content heart, listening as you increase our faith, never again behind

We had to PUSH

Then Jesus said to his disciples: If any of you want to be my followers, you must forget about yourself. You must take up your cross and follow me. (Matthew 16:24 CEV)

Written as God came to my rescue on, 2/32020 © Dr. Cynthia Locke Henderson

✎ God's word is powerful. What does this scripture say to you?

_____
_____
_____
_____
_____

✎ What have you learned during this time with Lord?

_____
_____
_____
_____
_____

✎ Are there things you need to do differently?

_____
_____
_____
_____
_____

✎ Before you leave this moment, write down God's directions to you.

_____
_____
_____
_____
_____

✎ Close this journaling moment with a prayer.

_____
_____
_____
_____
_____

Lord, Search My Heart And Thoughts

(PSALM 139:23)

Lord, you know what is hidden and unexposed in the heart of man and woman
You know there are things that we need to band or disrobe while taking a greater stand
Things that have been secrets from others but not a secret to you, things that we dare not scatter
Things that we protect believing as long as others don't see them, they do not matter

Lord, you know our thoughts and how we respond without saying a word
Thoughts that are unspoken, thoughts we guard and shelter because others have not heard
But you O Lord are cognizant of the feelings, beliefs and opinions hidden deep within our minds
You know before they are spoken, the danger they bring to us daring us to cross spiritual lines

Lord, we commit our heart and thoughts to you surrounding them for your removal and repair
Lord, change the bad thoughts made audible, change the thoughts spoken silently without any care
Bring transformation to the things that tear down your plans for our thoughts and hearts
Lord, do a renovation for those things that are not you and place us in line with a spiritual restart

Written during my time with God on February 27, 2019 by Dr. Cynthia Locke Henderson©

🖊 God's word is powerful. What does this scripture say to you?

_____
_____
_____
_____
_____

🖊 What have you learned during this time with Lord?

_____
_____
_____
_____
_____

🖊 Are there things you need to do differently?

_____
_____
_____
_____
_____

🖊 Before you leave this moment, write down God's directions to you.

_____
_____
_____
_____

🖊 Close this journaling moment with a prayer.

_____
_____
_____
_____
_____

Lord Teach Me Your Way

(PSALM 86:11)

Lord, I have walked my way and inconsistently walk in your truthful instruction
Finding my way of doing this has been consistently under construction
I need you to be my designer, my sculptor and my fortress building this relationship with you
Lord, I desire you to be the center of my life, my friend like no other, my consultant in all that I do

You have promised me that you would never leave me alone or forget about this person you fore knew
I may seem like I have it in control, I keep relying on other things and not your promises that's for sure
I put my confidence and my trust in what I think I know and what others seem to have solutions for
Repeatedly you restore and refresh because your promises mean more as you stand at my opened door

You never seem tired of me coming back asking for forgiveness and a second chance. You welcome me back
You promised to forgive my sins and no longer remember them. You allow me to start a clean forgiven track
Lord, unite my thoughts, my ways, and my heart to the plans you have for me
Lord, my desire is that You let this relationship we are building grow stronger between me and thee

Written during my time with God on February 28, 2019
by Dr. Cynthia Locke Henderson©

God's word is powerful. What does this scripture say to you?

_____

_____

_____

_____

_____

What have you learned during this time with Lord?

_____

_____

_____

_____

_____

Are there things you need to do differently?

_____

_____

_____

_____

_____

Before you leave this moment, write down God's directions to you.

_____

_____

_____

_____

_____

Close this journaling moment with a prayer.

_____

_____

_____

_____

_____

Cry Out To God For Purpose

(Psalm 37:2)

Lord, you are there always when I am in a state of self-investigation
Wondering what I've gone through and yet have to go through at this life
station
Within myself I reach a point of needing your clear and direct purpose
for me at a certain time
When I line up the battles, the victories, moments of inquiry I wonder
what's next in line

Deep within me I feel there is more that you want to see and be for me
Lord I cry out with discrepancy in my heart, Lord I know there is more,
hear my cry and plea
You have ordered my footsteps, that I can clearly see from birth to this
moment crying for you
Lord I am available to you, please tell me what's next, I need that from
you and not what I think I must do

Lord, you see, hear, know all, even the days that I cried silently within my
heart
You know the times that I felt I did not measure up to what others
thought should be my part
Lord, I surrender all that you have created in me, all that you gave as you
ordered my paths in life
I receive the steps that lie ahead of my expectation and yield myself to
the creation of your carving knife

Written during my time with God on March 1, 2019 by Dr. Cynthia Locke Henderson©

🖊 God's word is powerful. What does this scripture say to you?

_____

_____

_____

_____

_____

🖊 What have you learned during this time with Lord?

_____

_____

_____

_____

_____

🖊 Are there things you need to do differently?

_____

_____

_____

_____

_____

🖊 Before you leave this moment, write down God's directions to you.

_____

_____

_____

_____

_____

🖊 Close this journaling moment with a prayer.

_____

_____

_____

_____

_____

PTT Me
(Prove, Try, Test)

(PSALM 26:2)

Being able to recite your word is totally different from knowing and applying your word to my soul
So many years I have listen to sermons, read your words to know what was done in days of old
Lord, I need an upgrade, an examination of the actions in my life to find, you were there all the time
Pressures seemed unbearable, yet the flicker of your light clears my vision to see you are primary and prime

Lord, at times so many efforts were made to destroy my life, to challenge my faith in your promises to me
Pressures to make me feel empty, loss and standing on the edge of a cliff, however, you are my promise key
The world took things that mattered to me - family, relationships, position, and exhausted talents you gave
Feeling like a kinsman to Job, the end of this trying period led to restoration and validation that I was saved

You proved me to be yours, you tried me and did not let me disconnect, and then came the test
Would I serve you without the family, relationships, position and gifts, my answer is "YES" I will give my best
You restored me with greater things than before, you opened more doors than the world could close
I know that more PTT will come my way, Lord I trust you because I am the person you chose

Written during my time with God on March 2, 2019 by Dr. Cynthia Locke Henderson©

God's word is powerful. What does this scripture say to you?

_____

_____

_____

_____

_____

What have you learned during this time with Lord?

_____

_____

_____

_____

_____

Are there things you need to do differently?

_____

_____

_____

_____

_____

Before you leave this moment, write down God's directions to you.

_____

_____

_____

_____

_____

Close this journaling moment with a prayer.

_____

_____

_____

_____

_____

Daddy The Road Has So Many Turns, Crack, And Holes

(Psalm 143:10)

Daddy, I looked ahead as far as I could see feeling it was an easy trip
My view could only see a limited distance just before the road took a dip
Some things past that dip were not in my view, but I proceeded without consulting you
Relying on my strength, I could not imagine there would be things to block my getting through

Daddy, I did not see the turns that suggested a better route to get to where I wanted to go
I tried a few short cuts that only took me in wrong directions and made my trip longer and slow
I did not see the cracks that distracted my faith in you and refocused my directions for your plan
I totally missed seeing the holes that crippled me and nearly took my life and disabled my stand

Daddy, I now know that I cannot make it without your lead, the ground around me is unsteady
I need you now, I need you every second, minute, hour, day, week, month and year to help me be ready
You have plans for me that were put in place before I was created, before I acquired anything
Father God, lead me with your good Spirit to level ground because you O Lord are my King

Written during my time with God on March 4, 2019 by Dr. Cynthia Locke Henderson©

God's word is powerful. What does this scripture say to you?

_____

_____

_____

_____

_____

What have you learned during this time with Lord?

_____

_____

_____

_____

_____

Are there things you need to do differently?

_____

_____

_____

_____

_____

Before you leave this moment, write down God's directions to you.

_____

_____

_____

_____

_____

Close this journaling moment with a prayer.

_____

_____

_____

_____

_____

Lord, I Find Myself "Here". Help!

———— ·ᴥ·~ᴥ· ————

Lord, I do not grow weary of your love, your grace, your strength

I've learned the lessons of tests and trials over and over again

Each test I enter, you bring me through, I cannot make it without you

You direct my thoughts, my pain, my inquiry and help me know that I matter

The human elements of me bring tears when I thought I had run out of tears

The human elements of me tamper with my faith, I refuse to do nothing less than trust you

Lord, at this time, this moment I need you as my "cup" refreshing and restoring me with living waters

I need you to quench my thirst for direction from this place I find myself in

I need you to collect my tears in that cup while letting me know that you have saved everyone

As I drink from the cup, I remember the victory you gave in previous times of trial and test

I needed your directions then and I continue to need them now

I live by your promises and know you support my promises that are according to your will

Bless my seed and allow me to see your miraculous hand at work once again

I rest on your promise that you will never leave nor forsake me

I rest on your promise to give me the desires of my heart

Please know that my desire is first to do your will and that my desires are saturated with pleasing you

I am "here" and need assurance that you are "here" with me
You already know the intricate parts of my "here" situations
Underneath this physical and mental pain, I know you are there
I will not leave you; I just need to feel you in this "Here Place"
I will continue to walk towards you even when I don't see you
I will listen for you when all seems silent
I will cry out to you because I know you are listening
I know that when I am weak, then I am strong in you
You are my strength

Written during my time with God interceding for a friend,
on March 4, 2019 by Dr. Cynthia Locke Henderson©

✎ God's word is powerful. What does this scripture say to you?

_____

_____

_____

_____

_____

✎ What have you learned during this time with Lord?

_____

_____

_____

_____

_____

✎ Are there things you need to do differently?

_____

_____

_____

_____

_____

✎ Before you leave this moment, write down God's directions to you.

_____

_____

_____

_____

_____

✎ Close this journaling moment with a prayer.

_____

_____

_____

_____

_____

Here I Am

(EXODUS 3:4)

How amazing it is to feel your answers to my many calls
How amazing it is that you pick me up from so many falls
How amazing you are always ready and available to my call in the middle of my storm
How carefully you give hear and make me feel that I am important, I am on your platform

Lord, I feel so inadequate because I am not always available and ready to say "Here I Am"
I retreat feeling I am not worthy of your call and close myself like the shell on a clam
It is time for me to rest on your word that invites me to come just as I am without trying to fix me up
Lord, you have chosen me, you come to me without charge, you always extend your grace cup

Lord, my heart says, "Here I Am" yet my mind battles with my feelings that say I can't do it
I fear that I will not be able to handle what you send my way, I feel so unready and unfit
Then you remind me of tremendous battle of the past, situations where help seemed far away
Constantly you armed me with what I needed, Lord by faith I say, Here I am and with you I will stay

Written during my time with God on March 5, 2019 by Dr. Cynthia Locke Henderson©

God's word is powerful. What does this scripture say to you?

_____

_____

_____

_____

_____

What have you learned during this time with Lord?

_____

_____

_____

_____

_____

Are there things you need to do differently?

_____

_____

_____

_____

_____

Before you leave this moment, write down God's directions to you.

_____

_____

_____

_____

_____

Close this journaling moment with a prayer.

_____

_____

_____

_____

_____

Interruptions

(PSALM 51:12)

Lord, you give joy, you give peace, you give safety, you give strength, you give us your best
Lord, you give us tests that help us grow, tests that strengthen our faith, you also give some hard tests
In these tests you uphold us with a willing hand, you never abandon us, you have us under construction
Yet on our way to following your predestined plans for us we find ourselves in a sea filled with interruption

Taking on other's tests and the result of disobedience causes us to be distracted from what you are teaching us
Finding ourselves in the middle of tactics Satan designs to shift our focus and minimizing our trust
These interruptions cloud the promises of God to fight our battles and to keep our heart trouble free
We forget who is holding us up with his willing hand while providing a way of escape and directions to flee

Oh God, how we try to do things our way only to find it is best when you have done all you can, just stand
Battles will come as we wage spiritual warfare, situations will come that seem to alter what God planned
Just because we fall off the road on our way to the joy and peace that only God can give
He does not exit he remains there, telling us this interruption will not kill us, He promises that we will live

Written during my time with God on March 6, 2019 by Dr. Cynthia Locke Henderson©

God's word is powerful. What does this scripture say to you?

_____

_____

_____

_____

What have you learned during this time with Lord?

_____

_____

_____

_____

Are there things you need to do differently?

_____

_____

_____

_____

Before you leave this moment, write down God's directions to you.

_____

_____

_____

_____

Close this journaling moment with a prayer.

_____

_____

_____

_____

See Me, Show Me, Help Me

(PSALM 139:34)

What do I see when I really see me? What does God see when he looks at me through and through?

Can I admit that I am not the person I really think I am. Is what I show to God a vision that is true?

Am afraid to look at all sides of me, even the parts that I hide behind the mask?

Going behind that mask and pulling out that in my secret places, in my hidden treasure is an awesome task.

There are things and feelings that block me from my relationship with God and where he wants me to be.

Lord I want to be always available to you, I want the blockage to be exposed to me and removed is my plea.

Lord I am not looking for the gold at the end of the rainbow, I am looking for a better relationship with you.

I am willing to walk the path that's traveled by few. I want to be what you want, presentable for your view

I don't want to take your love, grace, mercy and strength for granted. At this point I need you more.

I committed to walking in the doors you opened, I have this thrust for you will that eats at my core.

Lord I know you see me better than I see myself, you have customized my path with designs for me

You have taken me through test, I have failed test, been retested, help me be blind spot free

Written during my time with God on March 7, 2019 by Dr. Cynthia Locke Henderson©

God's word is powerful. What does this scripture say to you?

_____

_____

_____

_____

What have you learned during this time with Lord?

_____

_____

_____

_____

Are there things you need to do differently?

_____

_____

_____

_____

Before you leave this moment, write down God's directions to you.

_____

_____

_____

_____

Close this journaling moment with a prayer.

_____

_____

_____

_____

_____

Whining Does Not Help

Unfair treatment does not give us to permission to whine
It does not move us up closer in God's line
It shows how little we trust God for certain infringements that make life challenging
We quickly forget God is King as we become overwhelmed in an earthly thing

We take the setbacks from unfairness and allow them to distract us from what God teaches
Our whining and moaning blocks from hearing God's promise, we move out of his reaches
He tries to reach us through his words, through our worship and praise
We don't even cry out to God because our anger is like an intensified blaze

Lord, you are a forgiving God when I move from my whining and my complaint
I find my way back to you "my dad and father", I pray and for spiritual constraint
Lord, thank you for showing me how unfairness can alter my thoughts and demonstration of belief
I have to bring my life challenges to you, then and only then can I get relief

Lord you bring the sun out and brighten up my day!

Written during my time with God on March 8, 2019 by Dr. Cynthia Locke Henderson©

_/_ God's word is powerful. What does this scripture say to you?

_____

_____

_____

_____

_____

_/_ What have you learned during this time with Lord?

_____

_____

_____

_____

_____

_/_ Are there things you need to do differently?

_____

_____

_____

_____

_____

_/_ Before you leave this moment, write down God's directions to you.

_____

_____

_____

_____

_____

_/_ Close this journaling moment with a prayer.

_____

_____

_____

_____

_____

Legacy

Grow from the legacy that Jesus left when he died for "ALL" who were lost
He left forgiveness, without a price tag because he paid it all on the cross
His legacy said that He would rather die than be without us
Leaving the legacy of eternal life with Him if we simply repent and trust

All those things that grow in us such as hate, bitterness, envy, selfishness, hurt from the past
Let them all go, they destroy your good legacy, throw those bad thoughts and feeling in the trash
Dig up the weeds of feelings of unfairness. Stop waiting for others to change, be the change you want to see
Asking God to create in you a clean heart, readies the field for you sow seeds of goodness that is the key

Allow God to use your life to glorify Him, to impact others by all the gifts and talents that He has given you
Show and tell the unmeasurable grace that He has given to you repeatedly, leaving bill showing nothing due
Leave a legacy that lives on without your life, that reminds others that you were chosen and purpose driven
Leave a legacy that confirms to others that no bad deeds are held against you because you are forgiven

Written during my time with God on March 9, 2019 by Dr. Cynthia Locke Henderson©

🖊 God's word is powerful. What does this scripture say to you?

_____
_____
_____
_____
_____

🖊 What have you learned during this time with Lord?

_____
_____
_____
_____
_____

🖊 Are there things you need to do differently?

_____
_____
_____
_____
_____

🖊 Before you leave this moment, write down God's directions to you.

_____
_____
_____
_____
_____

🖊 Close this journaling moment with a prayer.

_____
_____
_____
_____
_____

Light

(PSALM 34:3)

In the beginning God created heaven and the earth
Assigning each its value and worth
He commanded light to exist and separated it from darkness
Assigning light to day and darkness to night each had its own address

He created man during the creation of the universe
As the cycle unfolded man took on darkness opening the door to something worse
Darkness became the place where in man's heart that breaded deceit, wrath, lies, greed and sin
Today man has the option to stay in darkness or to accept God's invitation to light and win

God does not force himself on anyone, he invites you into the light it is your choice
Christ light shines in the dark places in your life and darkness no longer has a voice
God is aware of the darkness in you there is no need to hide it, release it
There are no prerequisites, Christ invites you to come as you are no one will be sent away

Ask Him, He will lead you to his holy hill and dwelling.
His light is there for you.

Written during my time with God on March 11, 2019 by Dr. Cynthia Locke Henderson©

God's word is powerful. What does this scripture say to you?

_____
_____
_____
_____
_____

What have you learned during this time with Lord?

_____
_____
_____
_____
_____

Are there things you need to do differently?

_____
_____
_____
_____
_____

Before you leave this moment, write down God's directions to you.

_____
_____
_____
_____
_____

Close this journaling moment with a prayer.

_____
_____
_____
_____
_____

The Value Of My Days

(PSALM 39:5)

Lord, by nature I am transitory, happy and peaceful at one point, and in and out of brokenness, pain.

What do I gain by assigning numbers to the days I have asked you to move or fix things for my gain?

My days are a few handbreadths and my lifetime numbers are nothing before you.

You give time to my life as you see fit. I stand as a mere breath to you who knows me through and through.

My focus needs to be on what I do with the days, weeks, months and years your breathed into my existence.

My focus needs to be on your saving grace that is forgiving, even through my disobedience and resistance.

I need to really realized that I can be here today and gone tomorrow, just a memory away!

A glimpse of my life reminds me of Gods mercy. Do I marinate on what could have been or for this day I pray?

My days have no value if I have wasted them on thing and thoughts that do not give life but tear me down.

Am I a Godly verb with actions that worships God? Have wasted so much time that I am a no action noun?

My memories have worth if I learned from experiences or have a testimony to share about God's deliverance

Every step I take, every breath I breathe makes it vital that I freely trust God and not give my days to chance

Written during my time with God on March 12, 13, 2019
by Dr. Cynthia Locke Henderson©

God's word is powerful. What does this scripture say to you?

_____

_____

_____

_____

_____

What have you learned during this time with Lord?

_____

_____

_____

_____

_____

Are there things you need to do differently?

_____

_____

_____

_____

_____

Before you leave this moment, write down God's directions to you.

_____

_____

_____

_____

_____

Close this journaling moment with a prayer.

_____

_____

_____

_____

_____

God, Send Me

(ISAIAH 6:8)

There is the power of life and death in the little pink thing that lies between our teeth in our mouth.

What is said out of our mouth has the power of life and death that reaches east, west, north and south.

God is aware of our apprehensions and fear to commit to the calls on our life, our mission, and our plan.

That is why we put on the full armor of God to ensure that against the devil's warfare we are able to stand.

Deep within your heart you feel you are not worthy to be sent by God. This is not true if God speaks to you.

Deep within your heart there rises a fear the you are not qualified to answer his call telling you what to do.

Those feelings are the first attack on your respond to say to God, "Here am I, send me", I will take the trip.

You are given the chance to answer, because God chose you. Whom he chooses he also qualifies and equip.

I was not created by me, God created me for a purpose, He foreknew all the directions of my life would go

My steps may not have always been good, yes there has been sin in my life, God knows me head to toe

My experiences allowed me to grow and, in my weakness, I have been made strong.

God you receive me just as I am because your blood makes it possible for me to go because to Him, I belong

Lord send me, I will go!

Written during my time with God on March 13, 2019 by Dr. Cynthia Locke Henderson©

🖊 God's word is powerful. What does this scripture say to you?

_____
_____
_____
_____
_____

🖊 What have you learned during this time with Lord?

_____
_____
_____
_____
_____

🖊 Are there things you need to do differently?

_____
_____
_____
_____
_____

🖊 Before you leave this moment, write down God's directions to you.

_____
_____
_____
_____
_____

🖊 Close this journaling moment with a prayer.

_____
_____
_____
_____
_____

God You Never Stopped Loving Me

(PSALM 119:135)

Lord, you never stopped loving me, even though it felt that way during difficult time.

Though my experiences took me through periods when what happened to me was a crime.

I held on to a very thin line of hope knowing that you were somewhere near.

How could I survive, would I survive, what would happen if I survived was my biggest fear?

Those periods were endured without the compassion of others, I could not share not even with my brother.

In the midst of that compassionless, aloneness, I could not even share with my mother.

There was no one in the space, but you O God, holding things together because I was coming apart.

Yet deep inside of my trying circumstances, there you were holding and preserving my heart.

I now look back to see that you had me, all of me, loving me like no one could ever imagine or think.

You knew how much I could take because, you had the power to make those circumstance go in one wink.

I now see that each one of those circumstance were lessons to reach others and to made me stronger.

Despite Satan's attempt to destroy my life you added volume and spiritual stamina to stay in the race longer.

Written during my time with God on March 14, 2019 by Dr. Cynthia Locke Henderson©

God's word is powerful. What does this scripture say to you?

_____

_____

_____

_____

_____

What have you learned during this time with Lord?

_____

_____

_____

_____

_____

Are there things you need to do differently?

_____

_____

_____

_____

_____

Before you leave this moment, write down God's directions to you.

_____

_____

_____

_____

_____

Close this journaling moment with a prayer.

_____

_____

_____

_____

_____

You Love Me Enough To Die For Me

(PSALM 51:1)

Thank you, Lord, for loving me enough to give your life for me
Thank you for helping me see the things about me that I could not see
Thank you for your mercy turns a blinded eye to the things that hold me down with guilt
Thank you for word that reassured me that you care, help me retain the restoration that you built

At this time and place in my life I release my fears a move forward where you want me to be
Lord, I listen to the strength you speak in your words that keep me focus on thee
Despair attempts to reroute me to a place of darkness and place where I can't see the value you see in me
Sin comes in all forms available, distractions, spiritual warfare making me feel like I am not free

I know that I am in your heart and with your hands of merciful, grace and strength
I know that you walk with me no matter how big my struggle, no matter its length
I rest in the peace of knowing that to you I matter, to you I have value
Behold you have taken away the old things that stop my progress, in your sight I am new

Written during my time with God on March 15, 2019 by Dr. Cynthia Locke Henderson©

God's word is powerful. What does this scripture say to you?

_____

_____

_____

_____

_____

What have you learned during this time with Lord?

_____

_____

_____

_____

Are there things you need to do differently?

_____

_____

_____

_____

Before you leave this moment, write down God's directions to you.

_____

_____

_____

_____

Close this journaling moment with a prayer.

_____

_____

_____

_____

_____

Lump Of Clay

———— ❦ ————

(ISAIAH 64:8)

In the potter's hand I was just a lump of clay formed from the basic material; dirt.

Subjected to life and all that comes in that package, love, hate, test, judgement, auditions, pain, hurt.

Can I become beautiful, would I be useful, did I have purpose, what would I be worth?

Am I just a lump of clay tossed about, why was I included on this place called earth?

Does the potter know that there are cracks in this vessel that he created?

Cracks from broken friendships, from broken promises and from feeling that I am hated?

Does the potter see the holes that are deep within deep, some big and some small?

Holes that came with punches of frustration, piercing anger, some hidden; can He see them all?

Yes, the potter sees all of the imperfections, but He also see the strength and beauty.

He cares and sees potentials of greatness for He is the potter that is His love duty.

We get anxious; however, we must realize that God is not finish with us yet.

Giving his life on Calvary was his payment for this lump of clay, that was His installment on sin debt.

Accept His crafting skills, let Him do the work in you, trust the hands that holding you!

Written during my time with God on March 16, 2019 by Dr. Cynthia Locke Henderson©

God's word is powerful. What does this scripture say to you?

_____

_____

_____

_____

_____

What have you learned during this time with Lord?

_____

_____

_____

_____

_____

Are there things you need to do differently?

_____

_____

_____

_____

_____

Before you leave this moment, write down God's directions to you.

_____

_____

_____

_____

_____

Close this journaling moment with a prayer.

_____

_____

_____

_____

_____

I Am Getting Old, But I Still Have Some Strength Left

(Psalm 71:9)

I have been around for a long time; some classify me as a senior or elder, while other say I am old age.

I am just thankful that God did not leave me in diapers, he has allowed me to grow and reach this stage.

To us we have been traveling through time and seen things come and go, we have seen birth and death.

Friends of our age leave many ways; traveling, or leaving to get support due to declining health.

We have survived, infancy, childhood, adolescent and some of us have arrived to adulthood.

Many of us now stand in places where our mothers and fathers once stood.

Reaching a status where younger children in our families see us as majestic because we are their grand.

Our seeds have multiplied, we give them tidbits of wisdom, and encourage them pursue a Godly stand.

We have acquired a lot of things; wisdom, experiences, history, generational stories told to us.

Take time, ask us questions about our days gone by, how we survived and learn to give God our trust.

We are old and "Arthur" visits frequently, but we still have some strength and time and a lot to share.

Making deposits in your lives while we can is our desire, we want your care and to show you, we care.

Written during my time with God on March 17, 2019 by Dr. Cynthia Locke Henderson©

God's word is powerful. What does this scripture say to you?

_____

_____

_____

_____

_____

What have you learned during this time with Lord?

_____

_____

_____

_____

_____

Are there things you need to do differently?

_____

_____

_____

_____

_____

Before you leave this moment, write down God's directions to you.

_____

_____

_____

_____

_____

Close this journaling moment with a prayer.

_____

_____

_____

_____

_____

Choosing God's Path

(PSALM 27:11)

As problems come face to face to me, I feel I can solve them
Without the wisdom of God, it is better if I leave things to Him
When decision that affect my walk with God, I cannot rest on my experience
My experiences have imperfections and does not always adhere to God's brilliance

Satan lurks and prowls 24/7 seeking whom he may destroy and devour
He is relentless and, in his efforts, seeks to rob you of the influence of God's power
We leave the path of God when we choose to take control based on our might
God warns us to wait on Him, he wants to teach us to be a level path that is right

Jeremiah 29:11, God has plans to prosper you and not to harm you, He wants you to live
God teach how to walk on level paths, His direction He will give, His joy he will give
If we wait, He will give us the right time and the exact response needed for circumstances
It is mandatory that we seek God and submit to his obedience and trust his chance

It was difficult writing this poem, just like it is difficult to do things God's way and not our way. I promise we will not be disappointed if we choose to follow God, starting today!

Written during my time with God on March 18, 2019 by Dr. Cynthia Locke Henderson©

God's word is powerful. What does this scripture say to you?

_____

_____

_____

_____

_____

What have you learned during this time with Lord?

_____

_____

_____

_____

_____

Are there things you need to do differently?

_____

_____

_____

_____

_____

Before you leave this moment, write down God's directions to you.

_____

_____

_____

_____

_____

Close this journaling moment with a prayer.

_____

_____

_____

_____

_____

Contentment With God

Daily reaching contentment with God is a goal continuously sought after
It is a place that only God can help me meet before the hereafter eternal life with the Master
Remove the lying that gives an appearance that all is well when my heart says that is not true
Remove the falsehood that merely present a fabricated picture to man, when God knows this is not you

Be anxious for nothing is what you directed us to do, therefore, we should not despise deficiency
All that we need you have O Lord, it is your desire that we not suffer lack because you have all sufficiency
It is first important that we seek righteousness so that, when we ask according to the will God, you hear us
Remove the desire of things that satisfies our prominence with man and removing request of lust

Lord, you know our name and everything that I need, help us to desire only what we need
Help us to not hunger for wealth that exceeds what we need and only fill us with greed
God created all and will supply our needs according to His riches in glory
Therefore, Lord help us to live with contentment in and focus living out you plans for our story

It was difficult writing this poem, just like it is difficult to do things God's way and not our way.

God is our father. Our daddy cares about us, our wants and needs.

I promise we will not be disappointed if we choose to follow God, starting today!

Written during my time with God on March 20, 2019 by Dr. Cynthia Locke Henderson©

God's word is powerful. What does this scripture say to you?

_____

_____

_____

_____

_____

What have you learned during this time with Lord?

_____

_____

_____

_____

_____

Are there things you need to do differently?

_____

_____

_____

_____

_____

Before you leave this moment, write down God's directions to you.

_____

_____

_____

_____

_____

Close this journaling moment with a prayer.

_____

_____

_____

_____

_____

Lord, I Hear You

Lord, you never left, you know my name, you know all there is to know about me. You chose me
My choices were altered, I did not always listen, I took my focus off of the reasons for your death at Calvary
I gave in to the crisis of struggle and focused with all my might to detour from the path you designed
I chose what I thought was easier, what I thought made more sense, and limited to what I intertwined

I reflect now and wonder if I had simply learned you, and built on our relationship together
No matter the storms that life brought my way, you were there saying fear not I control the stormy weather
You did not require any proof, yet you provide you love and provisions to me over and over repeatedly
You were there reaching out for me when things failed and I ended up crying out to you wanting to be free

Lord, you help me weather the storm, overcome the disappointments, recover from deceptions
Lord, as I waged worm in spiritual warfare, young rekindled my love for you geared me up with you weapons
Lord, the path wasn't straight, the way has sometime been harder than I could imagine, the valleys deep
Lord, I hear you because, you kept you promises to be my redeemer, my sustainer, I am yours to keep

Written during my time with God to build a closer relationship on March 21, 2019
by Dr. Cynthia Locke Henderson©

✏️ God's word is powerful. What does this scripture say to you?

_____

_____

_____

_____

_____

✏️ What have you learned during this time with Lord?

_____

_____

_____

_____

_____

✏️ Are there things you need to do differently?

_____

_____

_____

_____

_____

✏️ Before you leave this moment, write down God's directions to you.

_____

_____

_____

_____

_____

✏️ Close this journaling moment with a prayer.

_____

_____

_____

_____

_____

_____

Lord My Faith Without You Won't Work

Lord my faith without you will not get the job done, it just will not work.
I gone through so much trying to make things happen only to end up unnecessary hurt.
I am stepping out into unchartered territory
I have no clue Lord how this territory will affect my story

Thank you, Lord, for letting reach the point where I now know that you were there all the time
You let me fall so that I could know that you were there to catch my fall, heal the pain as you waited in line
You were there bottling up every tear that I shed
You were there all of those lonely moment as I lay in pain, hurt, aloneness on my troubled bed

Lord, thanks for only requiring only a mustard seed of faith from me to show me your power
Thank you for never leaving my side and stand as my fortress you were an all-surrounding tower
God you loved me when I thought I was unlovable; you were and still is my provision
And when the path is not clear and cloudy all I can see is you in my spiritual vision

Lord I have to have you because my faith will not work without you

Written during my time with God to build a closer relationship on March 21, 2019
by Dr. Cynthia Locke Henderson©

God's word is powerful. What does this scripture say to you?

_____

_____

_____

_____

_____

What have you learned during this time with Lord?

_____

_____

_____

_____

Are there things you need to do differently?

_____

_____

_____

_____

Before you leave this moment, write down God's directions to you.

_____

_____

_____

_____

Close this journaling moment with a prayer.

_____

_____

_____

_____

_____

Afterword

I have been traveling a distance from who I thought I was in Christ to a place of learning. It has been a seemingly long trip with difficult circumstances. It has been a trip that took me through the valleys in my life, through rough and rocky places only to get me to the even places. It took me through what felt like rivers of tears and hurt. However, God knew the right moments to bring me to dry land. The dry lands were another set of circumstances where I travel inside spaces that felt like nothing. Then in Philippians 4:13, he reminded me that "I can do all things through God who strengthens me". With that encouragement, I journeyed on to gradually climbing hills. The hills turned into mountains. These mountains seem to exceed my strength. At this point, I began to rely on God who needed me to learn from those mountainous experiences. Isaiah 41:10 "So do not fear, for I am with you; do not be dismayed, for I am your God. I will strengthen you and help you; I will uphold you with my righteous right hand." This living word spoke strength into me as continued the journey. Sometimes I had to climb and sometimes he gave me the strength needed to tunnel through.

Many journal entries later, I came to a place of intermission. God who has been with me on this journey gave me another word, ""Come to me, all you who are weary and burdened, and I will give you rest." Matthew 11:28. As I close this phase of my journey, my devotional music which is played by Dappy T Keys began playing "It is well with my soul". My God, what a journey I have been on! I have been on a prayer journey. I am not stopping. I am simply waiting for my next itinerary.

Scripture
Reference Versions

———— ❧ ————

BSB - Berean Study Bible

CEV - Contemporary English Version

ESV - English Standard Version

GNT - Good News Translation

KJV - King James Version

NASB 1995 - New American Standard Bible 1995

NKJV - New King James Version

NLT - New Living Translation

www.ingramcontent.com/pod-product-compliance
Lightning Source LLC
Chambersburg PA
CBHW021659120626
46545CB00004B/1321